DIGNIFIED DEPARTURE

Your Guide...
A Complete National
Outline For Preparing
All Neccesary Documents
To Control Your Death
Or That Of A Loved One

Bryane Miller

R & E Publishers

This book is sold with the understanding that the subject matter covered herein is of a general nature and does not constitute legal, accounting or other professional advice for any specific individual or situation. Anyone planning to take action in any of the areas that this book describes should, of course, seek professional advice from accountants, lawyers, tax and other advisers, as would be prudent and advisable under their given circumstances.

R&E Publishers
P.O. Box 2008, Saratoga, CA 95070
Tel: (408) 866-6303   Fax: (408) 866-0825

Book Design and Typesetting by elletro Productions
Book Cover by Kaye Quinn

ISBN 1-56875-059-5

Library of Congress Cataloging-in-Publication Data

Miller, Bryane K.
Dignified Departure : a complete national outline for preparing all necessary documents to control your death or that of a loved one / by Bryane K. Miller
    p. cm.
ISBN 1-56875-059-5 : $11.95
    1. Right to die--Law and legislation--United States. 2. Power of attorney--United States. 3. Right to die--Law and legislation--United States--States--Forms. 4. Power of attorney--United States--States--Forms. I Title
KF3827.E87M55 1993
346.73'029--dc20
[347.30629]
                                                        93-7541
                                                        CIP
Designed, typeset and totally manufactured in the United States of America.

INTRODUCTION

This book is dedicated to my late father, Dr. Carl Bryan Miller of Front Royal, Virginia, who died 10 July 1991 in the Lakeland Regional Medical Center in Lakeland, Florida. It is precisely because he was always so timely in addressing what was important that I hope people will use this as a guide for making out their own——

Advance Directives: a Living Will and a Durable Power of Attorney for Health Care document. My desire is that this will spare others the anguish of learning "too late" the legal complexities of Advance Directives and how they vary from state to state.

Although he had a "Living Will," my mother and I found it had no legal value to help us carry out his health care directives, because of Florida state statutes governing his particular condition. If my father had not passed away when he did at 5:30 a.m., we were to commence legal action at 10:00 a.m. that day to obtain a court order to block further assaults to his already tortured body.

We were given every encouragement to do so by the legal staff at Lakeland Regional Medical Center and his attending physician. A special review was given by the Lakeland Regional Medical Center's Legal Board in an attempt to seek a variance, because of the case's complexities. However, this was denied because it was decreed it would not be in accordance with Florida law.

My hope is that this book will serve as a key document to make legally possible a peaceful crossing for a new life from this transitory one for those unlocking death's door. Also important is my hope everyone may have the opportunity to be informed of their home state's statute on Advance Medical Directives. Citizens need to know the lawful implementation of their state's statute on them. Americans need to understand how their documented intentions will be adhered to when their death is imminent, wherever it occurs within these United States.

Two forms of Advance Medical Directives and how legal implementation varies from state to state within these United States are herein addressed. One is referred to as a "Living Will" (LW). It gives one's intended wishes, while yet living, and his or her personal desires as to what medically specified conditions would bring to conclusion their death, as legally defined. The other document designates an appointed director to see that the patient's specified instructions and expressed wishes for contingent situations are carried out by the person entrusted as their Durable Power of Attorney for Health Care (DPAHC).

As a physician dedicated to the full healing of his patients' mind, body, and spirit, my father would be so honored if his passing would spare any individual and their families the agony that results when legal bioethics do not blend with the implementation of a patient's Living Will. He would also be comforted knowing other families would be relieved of the dual burden of being left not just with a living will that is invalid, but with their loved one's life being reduced to nothing more than that of a vegetative invalid.

As the truly mobile society we are as a nation and within today's telescoped world, it is vital that everyone have a Living Will and a DPAHC. This is crucial for all living individuals, because of the fact that we all face certain death. When the time for our death has arrived, and all that is important to us and in us comes to an end, it should give peace to know that the closing of our life's chapter of living will be done our way for a dignified departure.

It would not have been possible for me to complete this endeavor without the love and support of my mother and the guidance of unique individuals who have been instrumental. Unfortunately, it is not possible to list all of the wonderful people who have guided me from start to finish with the writing of this book.

Dr. David N. Magazine was the chief physician on duty when my father was admitted to the hospital. His devoted personal interest and wonderful professional care endeared him to my mother and me. His knowledge and attentions to detail was in perfect order, but above all was his true concern for the very essence of the person and his family, although we had never previously met. He enabled my father to feel dignified as the time for his departure proceeded. The gift he gave was great for all.

My initial inspiration and encouragement to document this work I credit Ms. Susan L. Marr, Director of Risk Management for Lakeland Regional Medical Center.

Spiritual guidance and blessing of divine purpose has been ordained from the time of my father's illness to this day in the personage of the Rev. James P. Coleman, Rector of Saint David's Episcopal Church in Lakeland, Florida.

Assistance in my understanding of the corresponding legalities of bioethics in its broad spectrum and the magnificent foreword to this book belong to the Honorable Gerald E. McNally, District Court, 52nd Judicial District, County of Oakland, Michigan, who tried the first case involving the "suicide doctor," Jack Kervorkian.

Understandable, but also unfortunate, is the request I honor by not acknowledging two senatorial staffs who were of tremendous aid. Although they may not be named by state nor individually, they know how sincerely grateful I am for all that they did to help.

The proof reading of this book I was fortunate to have done by Mr. Edward T. Bromfield, whose experience and support were invaluable.

The masterful type set that has been given the presentation I am most thankful for the time and talents given by my friend, Mrs. Robert D. Poe.

FOREWORD

A problem can be created by beginning an article with the definition of the subject matter. On the one hand, the definition can be so broad and all inclusive as to be meaningless; on the other hand, if a definition is too narrow or limited, the writer is forever qualifying and expanding on it. Either approach can lead to frustration and confusion for the reader.

In spite of the risks involved in giving the definition, I am going to give you my definition of our laws. It has served me well, and I have found it accurate as well as flexible. It provides for the permanency of the law, as well as its growth and change. Obviously, this definition would only apply to the laws of the United States. The laws are the rules we choose to live by. We choose our laws in one of three ways.

(1) The ballot box proposition. This is not an effective way to make or change our laws. The first and last significant ballot box proposition that I recall in Michigan was approximately 16 to 18 years ago. This proposition required a 10-cent return on all beer and all soft beverage containers. The Michigan voters approved this proposition.

(2) The second way we make or change our laws is by electing representatives to State and Federal office. This is not an effective way to make or change our laws. It is not effective for a number of reasons. The elective term is frequently so brief, it does not provide the necessary time to think through legislation, and then implement successful legislation. The elected officials are so eager to reflect the positions of their constituents, that very little is ever accomplished.

(3) The real and dynamic way that our laws are made and changed is by our lifestyles, or the way we choose to live. These changes in lifestyle are usually called movements. At times, the existence of these movements is not clear until their goals are accomplished. The law responds to these movements. The law does not lead, it follows or reacts. We have a movement to pick up momentum and the alert lawyer or citizen will come into court, less frequently the legislature,

and point out that what we did yesterday was fine for yesterday, but now we need a legal change, a response to the new situation. If the argument is before a court, this is really judicial legislation. Most significant legal changes are accomplished by judicial legislation.

What I propose to do is briefly mention a few social movements and the legal system's response to these movements, and then point out how the right to die is just another movement. I repeat again, the law in no way created these movements, it just reacts or responds to them.

We have an enormous amount of legislation and judge made law prohibiting sexual and racial discrimination. These laws regulate areas including travel, lodging, restaurants, recreation, ownership of property, employment and jury duty. This vast body of laws and legal precedents did not cause the feminist or civil rights movements. The movements caused the legal changes. Identifying legal changes is rather easy compared to identifying what caused the movement in the first place. In the 1970's and 1980's, we had the social phenomenon of live-in boyfriend and girlfriend. This situation was highlighted in the California case of *Marvin versus Marvin*. The traditional legal position was that unmarrieds were living in an illegal relationship, that was without the benefit of a marriage contract. Since their relationship was illegal, the courts refused to help them. The court in *Marvin versus Marvin* recognized the popularity of the unmarried relationship, and responded by giving Ms. Marvin some palimony. Other states followed California, by allowing unmarrieds to use the court system, and a body of law has developed to regulate this relationship. The point is, the law responded to the new social phenomena. The law did not create this new relationship.

An illustration of the fact that the law follows or reacts rather than leads is found in the curb cuts that you will find in every city and town in Michigan. At every street corner, the sidewalk has been reduced to the level of the street. This reduction of the sidewalk to the street level is not for the skateboarders or bicyclists, but for the handicapped; more specifically for the handicapped who returned from the Vietnam War. We, as a country, have never been eager to help the handicapped, especially the handicapped veteran from the Vietnam War. Why then should we go to the expense of reducing the level of our sidewalks, requiring ramps and modified restrooms? The chain of events goes like this. Due to advances in medical technology, they survived and returned home. Once home, they got together in vocal groups and demanded the opportunity to vote, go to the restrooms in restaurants. The law responded by requiring handicapped facilities, curb cuts and handicapped parking. When a social movement begins, the law does not respond immediately. The movement must be clearly identified and have some momentum.

When the old way is no longer satisfactory, the alert citizen or lawyer will argue—generally before a court, less frequently before a legislative body—that a change is necessary. At times, something new will go unregulated for a long time, and only after many deaths and personal injuries will the legal system be prodded into changing.

The Mo-ped, a combination bicycle and motorscooter, illustrates this delay in regulation. For years, there was absolutely no regulation of the Mo-ped. There were no qualifications for the operator or permissible areas of operation. A four year old might be found operating a Mo-ped on extremely busy highways. After many deaths and injuries, the law finally responded with some regulation. The ultra-light airplane is another illustration of no regulation until we had many deaths, injuries, and disruptions of normal airplane traffic. The law was changed by the courts and legislature to regulate and eliminate the problem caused by the ultra-light airplane.

Due to space-age medical technology and advanced life-support systems, we now have the right-to-die movement. In addition to advanced medical technology, we have increased demands for self-determination and freedom of choice. People appear to have made religion a more personal expression and less are they looking to authority. The right-to-die can be called a movement just like the feminist movement or civil rights movement. Social and medical forces have come together to create the right-to-die movement, and the law must respond and give the citizenry some direction in this emerging area. If the law refuses to recognize the existence of the right-to-die movement, it could become a revolution. The right-to-die movement embraces the most profound and ultimate religious, spiritual and personal values. We must look to all of the humanistic and liberal disciplines to find the satisfactory response to the right-to-die movement.

The purpose of the law is to regulate human activity in this world. To distinguish between acceptable and unacceptable behavior; to permit the former and prohibit the latter. Assisted suicide reaches into the other world, takes one into the other world; therefore, by definition, the law is incapable of being the sole discipline. As a matter of fact, assisted suicide is when the law leaves off and religion, philosophy, art and music take over.

The enormity of this issue is almost frightening. I would like to conclude with a quote from Pico Della Mirandola:

"'In the midst of the world,' the creator said to Adam, 'I have placed thee, so thou couldst look around so much easier, and see all that is in it. I created thee as a being neither celestial nor earthy, neither mortal nor moulder and overcomer; thou canst degenerate to animal, and through thyself be reborn to godlike existence. Animals bring forth from the womb what they should have; the higher spirits, on the other hand, are from the beginning, or at least soon after, what they remain in all eternity. Thou alone hast power to develop and grow according to free will: in one word, thou hast the seeds of all-embracing life in thyself!'"

The Honorable Gerald E. McNally
District Court 52nd Judicial District,
County of Oakland, Michigan

Contents

CHAPTER ONE

CRUZAN VERSUS DIRECTOR, MISSOURI DEPARTMENT OF HEALTH

The United States Supreme Court upheld for the American citizens the Constitutional right to die, in the 1990 case of *Cruzan versus Director, Missouri Department of Health*. The case ruled that the Missourian, Nancy Cruzan, who had been in a vegetative coma for seven years, following an automobile accident, had the right to die. While common law dictated that competent patients always have the right to refuse any and all treatment, that right was frequently lost when a patient became comatose, unconscious, terminally ill, or otherwise unable to make his or her own decision. The responsibility, then, for this decision fell on others: family, friends, or care-givers. However, because of the fear of legal liability; disagreement among institutions and involved individuals; or because of moral objections, these decisions were reached only after litigation in state or, occasionally, federal courts. Approximately only 130 cases were altogether litigated covering the right to die, with the result being, in many, that medical treatment was withdrawn, while in others the result of efforts to have life-sustaining treatment withdrawn have been denied.

It was the *Cruzan* ruling which determined for the first time that it is the Constitutional right of Americans to exercise their will to cease living. Although the case gave Americans the Constitutional right to die, the Court's ruling simultaneously contradicted this right, by leaving it up to the individual states to set guidelines requiring "clear and convincing evidence" to authorize withdrawal of a feeding tube or other life-support systems. While oral evidence is not excluded, it is excruciatingly clear that written evidence is much preferred and has far greater authority should a case be resolved in court.

Despite verbal statements in Cruzan's tragic case, that she would not want to live as a vegetable and had her family's support for the feeding tube removal, these verbal statements did not fulfill the "show me state" of Missouri's requirements. The high Court's ruling upholding the Missouri Court's decision has the potentiality of bringing the state of misery into the lives of countless families whose loved ones are in varying forms of vegetative conditions.

Therefore, while the *Cruzan* ruling gave the recognition of the constitutional "right to die" as being somewhat consistent with many lower court rulings, the case seems to have established a broader right than had previously been provided by many states. The *Cruzan* ruling facilitates for a patient the instruction to be followed for the withdrawal of life-sustaining medical treatment. However, these statutes are generally limited in scope.

Accordingly, now, under the American umbrella of patient protection given by the 1990 Supreme Court ruling on *Cruzan*, a patient who leaves explicit instructions regarding his or her medical treatment may have the right to have these instructions enforced, even if these instructions go beyond what is sanctioned under state statute. However, the word "may" is the key operative. Thus, the extent of an individual's right to forego life-sustaining medical treatment will, at times, require an examination of both federal and state law.

Yet unfortunately, most Americans are, or say they are, "so busy under the sun" that they have not put up the American Umbrella of their patient-protection rights. Leaving written instructions in advance of the time when they will indeed be far below under the sun would so aid their physicians or loved ones in reaching these important decisions. In an organized effort to help facilitate citizens to correct this omission and to be fully educated in handling and having their personal affairs properly documented, the United States Congress has passed a law. It is designed to increase awareness of an individual's right to dictate his or her medical treatment through written instructions. This law is...

CHAPTER TWO

THE PATIENT SELF-DETERMINATION ACT (PSDA)

This law, known as the Patient Self-Determination Act (PSDA) has delivered for the public welfare the medical equivalent of the *Miranda Rights*. Those are the constitutional rights that police routinely recite to violators of the law at the time of arrest. While one's heart may inadvertently stop beating temporarily at the point of arrest, it is rare indeed this is followed by cardiac arrest. If this travesty of justice occurs, this law is designed to protect the patient's rights, just as the *Miranda Rights* are designed to protect the unconvicted citizen's rights.

The law requires that all adult patients entering Medicare/Medicaid-participating hospitals, nursing facilities, providers of home health care or personal care services, hospices, health-maintenance organizations (HMOs) and health-insuring organizations (HIOs) will have to be informed of their right to accept or refuse medical or surgical treatment. It states that the patient's right, under that facility's state law, to execute a Living Will and grant a durable power of attorney for his or her medical care to another individual will be honored.

The measure's purpose is to educate people about their rights to make decisions regarding their health care and how they want to have these decisions carried out in accordance with their wishes should they become incapacitated from seeing that it is done. These rights can be legally documented by completion of a:

    1)   Living Will - (LW)
               this is also referred to as a Treatment Directive; and a:

2) Durable Power of Attorney for Health Care
    Document (DPAHC)
    this is also referred to as an
    Appointment Directive.

Collectively, Living Wills/Treatment Directives and DPAHCs/Appointment Directives are referred to as Advance Directives. They are well named, because they allow you to make decisions in advance of any future medical treatment. One of our American rights is to say "yes" to treatment you want, or to say "no" to treatment you do not want.

PSDA was introduced in the 101st Congress on October 17, 1989. The principle sponsor in the Senate legislation (Senate Bill 1766) was U.S. Senator Jack Danforth (Republican of Missouri). Senator Danforth was joined by Senator Daniel Patrick Moynihan (Democrat of New York) as co-sponsor. United States Congressman Sander M. Levin (Democrat of Michigan) introduced the companion bill in the House of Representatives.

The proposal was referred to the Senate Committee on Finance. It was sent to this committee, because it has legislative jurisdiction over Medicare and Medicaid certified facilities.

Senators Danforth and Moynihan have long been, and still are, members of the Finance Committee. Senator Moynihan is, in fact, the second-ranking Democratic Committee member, with first-in-line being Senator Lloyd Benson (Democrat of Texas). Currently, Senator Moynihan is the Chairman of Social Security and Family Policy of the Finance Committee. Senator Danforth is the fourth-ranking Republican Committee member.

Senate Bill 1766 became a part of the final deficit reduction bill under House Resolution 5835 (H.R. 5835). It was passed on October 27, 1990.

The proposal was received at the White House on October 31, 1990. This, ironically, is what is known today as "Halloween." It was the hallowed eve that had as its purpose in its origin, according to religious tradition, the attempt to save souls. This is the very purpose of the PSDA.

President George H. Bush signed H.R. 5835 into law on November 5, 1990. The law is titled, "The Omnibus Budget Reconciliation Act of 1990" (OBRA 90). It is the five hundred and eighth law of the 101st Congress, and is also referred to as Public Law 101-508.

PSDA comes under two sections. The first is Section 4206, which reads:

Section 2	Table of Titles
Title IV	Medicare, Medicaid and other health related programs. (Pages 1388-30)
Part 3	Provisions relating to parts A and B. (Pages 1388-102)
Section 4206:	Medicare provider agreements assuring the implementation of a patient's right to participate in and direct health care decisions affecting the patient. (Pages 1388-115-117)

The second is under Section 4751, which is still under Section 2 and Title IV, but it reads:

Part 4	Miscellaneous (Pages 1388-170)
Subpart E	Miscellaneous (Pages 1388-204)
Section 4751:	Requirements for advanced directives under state plans for medical assistance. (Pages 1388-204-206)

The following is a copy of both sections.

Subpart E—Miscellaneous

SEC. 4751. REQUIREMENTS FOR ADVANCED DIRECTIVES UNDER STATE PLANS FOR MEDICAL ASSISTANCE.

(a) IN GENERAL,—Section 1902 (42 U.S.C. 1396a(a)), as amended by sections 4401(a)(2), 4601(d), 4701(a), 4711(a), and 4722 of this title, is amended—
(1) in subsection (a)—
(A) by striking "and" at the end of paragraph (55),

(B) by striking the period at the end of paragraph (56) and inserting "; and", and

(C) by inserting after paragraph (56) the following new paragraphs:

"(57) provide that each hospital, nursing facility, provider of home health care or personal care services, hospice program or health maintenance organization (as defined in section 1903(m)(1)(A)) receiving funds under the plan shall comply with the requirements of subsection (w):

"(58) provide that the State, acting through a State agency, association, or other private nonprofit entity, develop a written description of the law of the State (whether statutory or as recognized by the courts of the State) concerning advance directives that would be distributed by providers or organizations under the requirements of subsection (w)."; and

(2) by adding at the end the following new subsection: "(w)(1) For purposes of subsection (a)(57) and sections 1903(m)(1)(A) and 1919(c)(2)(E), the requirement of this subsection is that a provider or organization (as the case may be) maintain written policies and procedures with respect to all adult individuals receiving medical care by or through the provider or organization—

"(A) to provide written information to each such individual concerning—

"(i) an individual's rights under State law (whether statutory or as recognized by the courts of the State) to make decisions concerning such medical care, including the right to accept or refuse medical or surgical treatment and the right to formulate advance directives (as defined in paragraph (3)), and

"(ii) the provider's or organization's written policies respecting the implementation of such rights;

"(B) to document in the individual's medical record whether or not the individual has executed an advance directive;

"(C) not to condition the provision of care or otherwise discriminate against an individual based on whether or not the individual has executed an advance directive;

"(D) to ensure compliance with requirements of State law (whether statutory or as recognized by the courts of the State) respecting advance directives; and

"(E) to provide (individually or with others) for education for staff and the community on issues concerning advance directives.

Subparagraphs (C) shall not be construed as requiring the provision of care which conflicts with an advance directive.

"(2) The written information described in paragraph (1)(A) shall be provided to an adult individual—

"(A) in the case of a hospital, at the time of the individual's admission as an inpatient,

"(B) in the case of a nursing facility, at the time of the individual's admission as a resident,

"(C) in the case of a provider of home health care or personal care services, in advance of the individual coming under the care of the provider,

"(D) in the case of a hospice program, at the time of initial receipt of hospice care by the individual from the program, and

"(E) in the case of a health maintenance organization, at the time of enrollment of the individual with the organization.

"(3) Nothing in this section shall be construed to prohibit the application of a State law which allows for an objection on the basis of conscience for any health care provider or any agent of such provider which as a matter of conscience cannot implement an advance directive.".[51]

"(4) In this subsection, the term 'advance directive' means a written instruction, such as a living will or durable power of attorney for health care, recognized under State law (whether statutory or as recognized by the courts of the State) and relating to the provision of such care when the individual is incapacitated. [52]

(b) CONFORMING AMENDMENTS—

(1) Section 1903(m)(1)(A) (42 U.S.C. 1396B(m)(1)(a)) is amended—

(A) by inserting "meets the requirement of section 1902(w)" after "which" the first place it appears, and

(B) by inserting "meets the requirement of section 1902(a) and" after "which" the second place it appears.

(2) Section 1919(c)(2) of such Act (42 U.S.C. 1396r(c)(2)) is amended by adding at the end the following new subparagraph:

"(E) INFORMATION RESPECTING ADVANCE DIRECTIVES.—A nursing facility must comply with the requirement of section 1902(w) (relating to maintaining written policies and procedures respecting advance directives).".

(c) EFFECTIVE DATE.—The amendments made by this section shall apply with respect to services furnished on or after the first day of the first month beginning more than 1 year after the date of the enactment of this Act.

(d) PUBLIC EDUCATION CAMPAIGN.—

(1) IN GENERAL.—The secretary, no later than 6 months after the date of enactment of this section, shall develop and implement a national campaign to inform the public of the option to execute advance directives and of a patient's right to participate and direct health care decisions.

(2) DEVELOPMENT AND DISTRIBUTION OF INFORMATION.—The Secretary shall develop or approve nationwide informational materials that would be distributed by providers under the requirements of this section, to inform the public and the medical and legal profession of each person's right to make

decisions concerning medical care, including the right to accept or refuse medical or surgical treatment, and the existence of advance directives.

(3) PROVIDING ASSISTANCE TO STATES.—The Secretary shall assist appropriate State agencies, associations, or other private entities in developing the State-specific documents that would be distributed by providers under the requirements of this section. The Secretary shall further assist appropriate State agencies, associations, or other private entities in ensuring that providers are provided a copy of the documents that are to be distributed under the requirements of the section.

(4) DUTIES OF SECRETARY.—The secretary shall mail information to Social Security recipients, add a page to the medicare handbook with respect to the provisions of this section.

SEC. 4752. IMPROVEMENT IN QUALITY OF PHYSICIAN SERVICES.

(a) USE OF UNIQUE PHYSICIAN IDENTIFIERS.—

(1) ESTABLISHMENT OF SYSTEM.—

(A) IN GENERAL.—Section 1902 (42 U.S.C. 1396(a) as amended by sections 4601(d), 4701(a), 4711(a), 4722(a), and 4751(a) is further amended by adding at the end the following new subsection:

"(x) The Secretary shall establish a system, for implementation by not later than July 1, 1991, which provides for a unique identifier for each physician who furnishes services for which payment may be made under a State plan approved under this title.".

(B) DEADLINE AND CONSIDERATIONS.—The system established under the amendment made by subparagraph (A) may be the same as, or different from, the system established under section 9202(g) of the Consolidated Omnibus Budget Reconciliation Act of 1985.

(2) REQUIRING INCLUSION WITH CLAIMS.—section 1903(i)(42 U.S.C. 1396b(i)), as amended by this title, is amended—

(A) by striking the period at the end of paragraph (11) and inserting "; or", and

(B) by inserting after paragraph (11) the following new paragraph:

"(12) with respect to any amount expended for physicians' services furnished on or after the first day of the first quarter beginning more than 60 days after the date of establishment of the physician identifier system under section 1902(x), unless the claim for the services includes the unique physician identifier provided under such system.".

(b) MAINTENANCE OF ENCOUNTER DATA BY HEALTH MAINTENANCE ORGANIZATIONS.—

(1) IN GENERAL.—Section 1903(m)(2)(A) (42 U.S.C. 1396b(m)(2)(A)), as amended by this title, is amended—

(A) by striking "and" at the end of clause (ix),

(B) by striking the period at the end of clause (x) and inserting "; and", and

(C) by adding at the end the following new clause:

"(xi) such contract provides for maintenance of sufficient patient encounter data to identify the physician who delivers services to patients.".

(2) EFFECTIVE DATE.—The amendments made by paragraph (1) shall apply to contact years beginning after the date of the establishment of the system described in section 1902(x) of the Social Security Act.

(c) MAINTENANCE OF LIST OF PHYSICIANS BY STATES.—

(1) IN GENERAL.—Section 1902(a)(42 U.S.C. 1396a(a)), as amended by this title, is further amended—

(A) by striking "and" at the end of paragraph (56),

(B) by striking the period at the end of paragraph (57) and inserting "; and", and

(B) EFFECTIVE DATE.—The amendments made by subparagraph (A) shall take effect as if included in the enactment of the Omnibus Budget Reconciliation[22] Act of 1989.

(2) CLARIFICATION OF APPLICATION OF CRITERIA FOR DENIAL OF PAYMENT.—

(A) IN GENERAL.—Section 1154(a)(2) (42 U.S.C. 1320c-3(a)(2)) is amended by striking the third sentence and inserting the following: "The organization shall identify cases for which payment should not be made by reason of paragraph (1)(B) only through the use of criteria developed pursuant to guidelines established by the Secretary.".

(B) EFFECTIVE DATE.—The amendment made by subparagraph (A) shall take effect as if included in the enactment of the Consolidated Omnibus Budget Reconciliation Act of 1985.

SEC. 4206. MEDICARE PROVIDER AGREEMENTS ASSURING THE IMPLEMENTATION OF A PATIENT'S RIGHT TO PARTICIPATE IN AND DIRECT HEALTH CARE DECISIONS AFFECTING THE PATIENT.

(a) IN GENERAL.—Section 1866(a)(1) (42 U.S.C. 1395cc(a)(1)) is amended—

(1) in subsection (a)(1)—

(A) by striking "and" at the end of subparagraph (O),

(B) by striking the period at the end of subparagraph (P) and inserting ", and", and

(C) by inserting after subparagraph (P) the following new subparagraph:

"(Q) in the case of hospitals, skilled nursing facilities, home health agencies, and hospice programs, to comply with the requirement of subsection (f) (relating to maintaining written policies and procedures respecting advance directives).": and

(2) by inserting after subsection (e) the following new subsection:

"(f)(1) For purposes of subsection (a)(1)(Q) and sections 1819(c)(2)(E), 1833(r), 1876(c)(8), and 1891(A((6), the requirement of this subsection is that a provider of services or prepaid or eligible organization (as the case may be) maintain written polices and procedures with respect to all adult individuals receiving medical care by or through the provider or organization—

"(A) to provide written information to each such individual concerning—

"(i) an individual's rights under State law (whether statutory or as recognized by the courts of the State) to make decisions concerning such medical care, including the right to accept or refuse medical or surgical treatment and the right to formulate advance directives (as defined in paragraph (3)), and

"(ii) the written policies of the provider or organization respecting the implementation of such rights;

"(B) to document in the individual's medical record whether or not the individual has executed an advance directive;

"(C) not to condition the provision of care or otherwise discriminate against an individual based on whether or not the individual has executed an advance directive;

"(D) to ensure compliance with requirements of State law (whether statutory or as recognized by the courts of the State) respecting advance directives at facilities of the provider or organization; and

"(E) to provide (individually or with others) for education for staff and the community on issues concerning advance directives.

Subparagraph (C) shall not be construed as requiring the provision of care which conflicts with an advance directive.

"(2) The written information described in paragraph (1)(A) shall be provided to an adult individual—

"(A) in the case of a hospital, at the time of the individual's admission as an inpatient,

"(B) in the case of a skilled nursing facility, at the time of the individual's admission as a resident,

"(C) in the case of a home health agency, in advance of the individual coming under the care of the agency,

"(D) in the case of a hospice program, at the time of initial receipt of hospice care by the individual from the program, and

"(E) in the case of an eligible organization (as defined in section 1876(b)) or an organization provided payments under section 1833(a)(1)(A), at the time of enrollment of the individual with the organization.

"(3) In this subsection, the term 'advance directive' means a written instruction, such as a living will or durable power of attorney for health care, recognized by the courts of the State) and relating to the provision of such care when the individual is incapacitated.".

(b) APPLICATION TO PREPAID ORGANIZATIONS.—

(1) ELIGIBLE ORGANIZATIONS.—Section 1876(c) of such Act (42 U.S.C. 1395mm(c)) is amended by adding at the end the following new paragraph:

"(8) A contract under this section shall provide that the eligible organization shall meet the requirement of section 1866(f) (relating to maintaining written policies and procedures respecting advance directives).".

(2) OTHER PREPAID ORGANIZATIONS.—Section 1833 of such Act (42 U.S.C. 13951) is amended by adding at the end the following new subsection:

"(r) The Secretary may not provide for payment under subsection (a)(1)(A) with respect to an organization unless the organization provides assurances satisfactory to the Secretary that the organization meets the requirement of section 1866(f) (relating to maintaining written policies and procedures respecting advance directives).".

(c) EFFECTIVE ON STATE LAW.—Nothing in subsections (a) and (b) shall be construed to prohibit the application of a State law which allows for an objection on the basis of conscience for any health care provider or any agent of such provider which, as a matter of conscience, cannot implement an advance directive.

(d) CONFORMING AMENDMENTS.—

(1) Section 1819(c)(1) of such Act (42 U.S.C. 1395i-3(c)(1)) is amended by adding at the end the following new subparagraph:

"(E) INFORMATION RESPECTING ADVANCE DIRECTIVES.—A skilled nursing facility must comply with the requirement of section 1866(f) (relating to maintaining written policies and procedures respecting advance directives).".

(2) Section 1891(a) of such Act (42 U.S.C. 1395bbb(a)) is amended by adding at the end the following:

"(6) The agency complies with the requirement of section 1866(f) (relating to maintaining written policies and procedures respecting advance directives).".

(e) EFFECTIVE DATES.—

(1) The amendments made by subsections (a) and (d) shall apply with respect to services furnished on or after the first day of the first month beginning more than 1 year after the date of the enactment of this Act.

(2) The amendments made by subsection (b) shall apply to contracts under section 1876 of the Social Security Act and payments under section 1833(a)(1)(A) of such Act as of first day of the first month beginning more than 1 year after the date of the enactment of this Act.

SEC. 4027. MISCELLANEOUS AND TECHNICAL PROVISIONS RELATING TO PARTS A AND B.

(a) HOSPITAL AND PHYSICIAN OBLIGATIONS WITH RESPECT TO EMERGENCY MEDICAL CONDITIONS.—

(1) PEER REVIEW.—(A) Section 1867(d) (42 U.S.C. 1395dd(d)), as amended by section 4008(b)(3), is amended by adding at the end the following new paragraph:

"(3) CONSULTATION WITH PEER REVIEW ORGANIZATIONS.—In considering allegations of violations of the requirements of this section in imposing sanctions under paragraph (1), the Secretary shall request the appropriate utilization and quality control peer review organization (with a contract under Part B of title XI) to assess whether the individual involved had an emergency medical condition which had not been stabilized, and provide a report on its findings. Except in the case in which a delay would jeopardize the health or safety of individuals, the Secretary shall request such a review before effecting a sanction under paragraph (1) and shall provide a period of at least 60 days for such review.[23]

(B) Section 1154(a) (42 U.S.C. 1320c-4(a)) is amended by adding at the end the following new paragraph:

"(16) The organization shall provide for a review and report to the Secretary when requested by the Secretary under section 1867(d)(3). The organization shall provide reasonable notice of the review to the physician and hospital involved. Within the time period permitted by the Secretary, the organization shall provide a reasonable opportunity for discussion with the physician and hospital involved, and an opportunity for the physician and hospital to submit additional information, before issuing its report to the Secretary under such section.".

(C) The amendment made by subparagraph (A) shall take effect on the first day of the first month beginning more than 60 days after the date of the enactment of this Act. The amendment made by subparagraph (B) shall apply to contracts under part B of title XI of the Social Security Act as of the first day of the first month beginning more than 60 days after the date of the enactment of this Act.

(2) CIVIL MONETARY PENALTIES.—Section 1867(d)(2)(B) (42 U.S.C. 1395dd(d)(2)(B)) is amended by striking "knowingly" and inserting "negligently".

(3) EXCLUSION.—Section 1867(d)(2)(B) (42 U.S.C. 1395dd(d)(2)(B)) is amended by striking "knowing and willful or negligent" and inserting "is gross and flagrant or is repeated".

THIS IS A SUMMARY OF WHAT PSDA REQUIRES THAT MEDICARE AND MEDICAID CERTIFIED FACILITIES MUST DO:

1) **Maintain** written policies and procedures concerning an individual's rights under state law (whether statutory or recognized by the courts of the

state) to make decisions concerning his or her care. These rights, according to state law, would include:

    (A)   The decision to accept or refuse medical or surgical treatment.

    (B)   The decision to formulate advance directives recognized under state law, such as through:

        u Written instructions about health care, as in the form of a Living Will. These written instructions are also known as Treatment Directives.

        u The appointment of an agent or surrogate to make health care decisions on the patient's behalf (Durable Power of Attorney for Health Care - DPAHC). These written instructions are also known as Appointment Directives.

2)   **Determine** that these written policies and procedures concerning an individual's rights for his or her health care decision making is provided to adult patients. These policies and procedures must be explained:

    (A)   At the time of admission, either as a hospital inpatient or as an outpatient;

    (B)   At point of admission as a resident of a skilled nursing facility;

    (C)   In advance of coming under care with a home health agency or hospice; or

    (D)   Upon enrollment in a health maintenance organization receiving federal funds.

3)   **Document** in the patient's medical records, whether or not an advance directive has been made by the patient.

4)   **Guarantee** not to condition the provision of care or otherwise discriminate against any individual based upon whether or not they may have an advance directive.

5)   **Ensure** compliance with advance directives consistent with state law respecting them at facilities of Medicare and Medicaid provider organizations.

6)   ***Provide*** for the education of staff (individually or with others) and the community on issues concerning advance directives.

THIS IS A SUMMARY OF WHAT PSDA DOES NOT DO:

1) It does not create any new rights.

2) It does not state any position on any specific decisions people may have the need to make.

3) It does not make it a law that people must document advance directives—either a Living Will or DPAHC.

4) It does not start a new trend.

Forty-four states now have some form of legislation on advance directives. Indeed, the concept of advance directives is widely supported, according to opinion polls that show an 80- to 90-percent favorable attitude from the public. However, while the concept is approved, only about 10 percent of mentally competent adults have signed a Living Will, and an even smaller number have designated someone else to make decisions as their Durable Power of Attorney for Health Care.

Advance Directives have been endorsed by:
◆ The American Association of Retired Persons
◆ The American Bar Association
◆ The American Chiropractic Association
◆ The American Hospital Association
◆ The American Jewish Committee
◆ The American Medical Association
◆ The Catholic Health Association
◆ The National Council of Churches
◆ The President's Commission for the Study of Ethical Problems in Medicine (1983)

The reason the Patient Self-Determination Act was so necessary is that our health care system has become overzealous with achieving life's continuum. At times, in so doing, the system has taken away the rights of patients and failed to give true compassion in caring for the patient's medical needs. Indeed, at times while medical care is plentiful, it is sympathy that has been rationed out by "the system."

The rationing of sympathy is not from the many wonderful doctors and nurses, who have to carry out federal and state laws, as well as the practice of good medicine. Sympathy is minutely rationed by the bureaucratic "system" of legal requirements, under whose auspices doctors and nurses must most literally operate.

Times and life's timetable have both drastically changed. In olden times people died at home. They were surrounded by loved ones who helped assure them of a peaceful crossing through death's door. The dying were loved and lauded for their individual essence, personal moral legacy, life's accomplishments and contributions to others, and role and position to loved ones.

Today, of the approximately two million people who die every year, 80 percent die in hospitals; and perhaps 70 percent of those die after the decision to forego life-saving measures. The percentage of deaths that occur today within the home is obviously small.

Today, society's viewpoint of this is as a most accepted practice. Childbirth today is generally also an institutionalized transmittal. We have become so inundated with factual accountings and a general sterile approach to life, that it is almost admirable that any of life's experience is outside of any of the various forms of "institutional" facilities.

An increasing percentage of people spend the last of life's winter in nursing homes. So now we have added another socially acceptable institutionalized period to be sandwiched within life's slices of cheese. If we continue, there will be so many holes in the chunk of life we are given that even the Swiss would be hard-pressed to recognize it.

The common place of the majority of death's occurrence today being in an institutional-type facility, necessitated the right of people to make their own decisions as outlined by the Patient Self-Determination Act. The PSDA also serves to improve communication among patients, their loved ones, and doctors. In many cases it will ease the burden on loved ones and health care providers at the time of death's impending occurrence. Feelings of guilt should be lessened when the time for decision arrives. This is whether or not there should be medical pursuit of all treatment, and it has been pre-outlined by the patient what they want.

Doctors' fear of liability and malpractice suits have many times caused their refusal of treatment termination, even when loved ones have said that medical intervention is the last thing in the world that their loved one would have wanted. Cases in which a patient's desires are not known to their loved ones, and thus most certainly to the attending physician, have generated tremendous speculation on the part of the patient's support system in their effort to best carry out the awesome responsibility of unspecified choices.

Personal dignity and autonomy is violated when an individual's decisions are made by someone else. The persons deciding what is best for anyone other than for themselves should become worried and very burdened. Advance directives do not solve all of the problems or answer all of the excruciatingly difficult questions of spider-web ethics which ultimately surface with terminal cases.

However, "advance directives" do give to the medical staff and the patient's loved ones just what the term states. They direct, in advance—of the terminal conditions of the patient—their instructions for their care. By having the person's choices made known, their loved ones sense of burden, pain and guilt should be assuaged. By not having an individual's choices outlined in advance might be interpreted as deliberate to insure nothing would be spared to keep you alive.

It is hoped that by having the PSDA, that the medical treatment patients receive will be viewed as more humane and effective because:

- ◆ Patients will know more about their treatment;
- ◆ Patients will be more involved in their treatment;
- ◆ Patient/doctor communication and mutual decisions will be increased; and that
- ◆ Tragic cases like Cruzan's might be avoided when patients are educated how they might state their desires more clearly.

The new responsibilities for Medicare or Medicaid providers commenced December 1, 1991 and are now monitored by the Health Care Financing Administration (HCFA) of the U.S. Department of Health and Human Services (HHS).

HHS was to initiate a nationwide public education campaign in regard to advance directives. The Department was to develop informational materials of the individual's right to refuse medical treatment and to complete advance directives. The educational material originated by HHS was to be in all Social Security mailings and to all Medicare/ Medicaid recipients.

Now, however, while the Patient Self-Determination Act information is to be covered in the new Medicare handbook, it will only be mailed to new Medicare/Medicaid recipients. The HHS was also originally to assist states in developing written information on individual state law regarding advance directives and help with writing state statutes, if so required. Now, the U.S. Department of Health and Human Services will do so, but only on a request basis, with the weight of responsibility being on the individual state.

The national deficit and overall money squeeze is the reason that federal funding to cover the full cost of implementation of the PSDA will be primarily up to Medicare/Medicaid funded facilities to coordinate individually. However, matching federal funds are available to the states upon request. It must be clearly understood that if the various facilities fail to comply, the ultimate penalty is that they will lose their licensing and funding as a Medicare/Medicaid provider.

Stated in its simplest terms, then: the implementation of PSDA is up to the specific facility and each state. The Department of Health and Human Services will be serving more as a resource and guard dog rather than as a participant and eager companionable mate.

Let us now address how facilities, in general, and hospitals, in particular, will actually go about presentation of the PSDA information. Admittedly, in theory, the Patient Self-Determination Act is a sound and a vitally needed rite. However, in general, the track record and approach that most hospitals have for informing the public of their rights as patients is rather bleak.

Usually, patients are just handed several forms to sign at the point of admission. This is done usually with very limited, if any, explanation.

Your deliverance of advanced directives, like one-way vehicle rental, does not cover your return passage. It is written to specify under what conditions you do not wish to return.

But often, one of these hospital admission forms states that the hospital can do anything that they want. So the question is: How will hospitals make patients comfortable with the idea that they are to make this most important decision?

"Competent patients" clearly have the indisputable right to refuse any and all treatment outlined for them, even if so doing would certainly hasten death. Patients who became comatose, unconscious, terminally ill, or otherwise unable to make decisions, had no legislation that sought to protect their rights prior to the Patient Self-Determination Act.

However, by giving people the guarantee of all of this information, the PSDA provides the optimum of hope that all people will request Living Wills. Unfortunately, many people will exercise their right to table their decision. They will say this until they have either consciously, or otherwise, so reached a conclusion with which they are comfortable. And some people will say that they just don't want to think about it at all.

The consequential situations that can, and often do, occur have long-reaching effects. These effects are on those who can least afford them, as well as on those who do have the feeling that they are financially secure. When we use the words "afford" and "secure," the application can be affirmative or negative when we are assessing our bank accounts. The question, however, is: Do the same answers apply when we are defining our emotional account in regard to this whole process? If the problem is with our emotions, then who is there who will help us to resolve these important questions?

People are often able to decide quickly if they want a private or semi-private room. This is usually a question of basic economics. Individuals will state, matter-of-factly, their preference for Kosher, salt-free, sugar-free, or vegetarian diets. These same individuals may deliberate for a long time over simple food choices within the selected categories.

Therefore, the problem not only becomes how people will make these critical decisions, but are people ready to make them?

If people are not ready now, when and what will the consequences be for not only them, and sometimes, more importantly, to those who love them, if they do not document these decisions? The choice that is not documented might be its own vote, although not the patient's desire.

It is by taking the first step achieved by this federal legislation requirement, the PSDA, that Medicare and Medicaid providers inform patients of a legal way to predetermine the manner and degree of their life's sustaining support through having...

CHAPTER THREE

"A LIVING WILL"

It has become a rather routine statement and accepted fact that: "we are a mobile society." We do now, by car, train, boat and plane, cross geographical boundaries separating the states within these United States of America. This is a routine occurrence, especially in our large metropolitan areas where individual commuters, and individuals who are touring and shopping, as well as those in the daily course of doing their job, often cross in one day a total of six or more state lines.

Our ability, both as individuals and as a population, to travel has enlarged our horizons for experience, bringing countless positive opportunities. At the same time this new ease by which we not only travel, but by which we are also influenced in our mental outlook, that is so integral to each individual's life, is rather uniformly accepted. Initially, the phrase "mobile society" was in specific reference to the automobile and the ease it gave in our lives for people to be able to get from one place to another.

In the beginning the people who enjoyed the benefits of this advanced technology giving "ease" to travel, which had before been an involved procedure, were people of some financial means who could afford to buy an automobile. It was these people of "means" who also usually maintained a certain standard of living and were categorically referred to as "society people" because they participated in social activities, usually just with one another. When exclusivity exits, or seems to exist, resentment that is felt on behalf of those who feel they are left out results in defining various categories.

Today's "new society" is composed of all people, and some families indeed do go back to "old society." It is also mobile and highly technical. We want to do a lot, be knowledgeable, and have a lot. Actually, our technology has flourished to the point of everything from car phones to the fact we no longer have to get in our cars to go even to the movies, unless we so desire, because we can see movies right at home on our VCRs.

All of this available ease to our approach and the actual means of our method of travel has not uniformly or appropriately elevated the general American awareness of the increased legal ramifications that technical advancement has created. This ease has made very basic every citizen's need to have records, both financial and personal, current and complete.

It is imperative that every citizen know exactly what his or her state statute is on "Living Wills," which are also referred to as Treatment Directives. Any number of considerations may shape the actual directive form and some states go so far as to prescribe certain forms, which, by law, a person may/ must use to have their desired medical treatment implemented.

While compliance with these laws requires an understanding of them and being educated as to their very existence, the effectiveness of them is analogous to automobile seat belts. These laws cannot help us if we don't "buckle-up."

The State of Virginia has adopted and publicized the slogan "Buckle-Up Virginia, It's the Law." "It is a law we can live with." Indeed, it is a law we oftentimes would not be alive without, because it saves lives in what could otherwise be fatal car accidents.

Present federal or state law does not mandate anyone must have a Living Will. However, TO HAVE A FEDERALLY APPROVED, UNIFORM LIVING WILL STATUTE THAT CITIZENS OF ALL STATES COULD SIGN WOULD SIMPLIFY WHAT CAN BECOME A FINANCIAL AND MEDICAL SPIDER-WEB NIGHTMARE IN ITS ABSENCE. Perhaps the federal government and all of our state governments should "go back to 'Ole Virginny,'" and adapt the slogan to: "SIGN A LIVING WILL—IT'S THE LAW" . . . . . "A LAW WE CAN'T LIVE OR DIE, AT PEACE, WITHOUT."

Some people say that having a law requiring a Living Will is a law we could die with. The fact is that while correct, the difference is that we would die as we so chose, not how it was medically and religiously ordained for us as "correct."

It is important that people remember that laws and documents do not create rights. People have the right to make decisions about their own care. The intent of having the Patient Self-Determination Act is to require patients to be informed about Treatment Directives/Living Wills and Appointment Directives/Durable Power of Attorney for Health Care documents and to remind people of what the law provides. Indeed, these written tools are to be the patient's insurance that his or her choice for health care is respected.

The very fact that an individual would have a signed Living Will should bring peace. They should know they could live without fear of their worst nightmare being realized—that is to be a helpless patient entangled in a spider web of medical state laws intertwined with moral threads, all woven into one deadlocked maze.

We have some choices to make in how we live. Most certainly, each one of us, can determine the moral conduct of our lives. It may be almost as important that we exercise our personal choice as to how we die. But, it needs to be fully understood and discussed with family, loved ones, clergy, and physicians.

As the story and song line goes:
"And the living was good,
And the living was easy."

Well, often, unfortunately for some, neither are consistently true. Certainly, everyone has some pain in life. The hope always is that we will have more good days than bad to live. Let us pray that the closing line for each of us will be:
"And the dying was good,
And the dying was easy."

The question often asked is: "As an individual with my own Living Will, am I assured my directions for my life not to be prolonged if my death seems imminent will be followed?" Unfortunately, the answer is "No, not necessarily." There is a potentially grave misconception that just having our Living Will spares us and our loved ones of the pain on our journey to the grave.

Inadvertently, the *Cruzan* ruling gave many people the erroneous impression that since they have a Living Will their wishes will be honored. Many people believe that just by having a Living Will they will not have Nancy Cruzan's twilight existence. In most states, a Living Will can only be put to use when a patient faces a terminal illness.

It is the definition of what constitutes a terminal illness that must be clear. "A terminal illness is a condition in which death is imminent in days, weeks or months, and usually is certified by two separate doctors."

Many states have statutes that authorize citizens to execute a Living Will or Treatment Directive instructing the withholding or withdrawal of life-sustaining procedures. However, these statutes are often only applicable when the individual, who is sometimes referred to as the "declarant" or "principal," is terminally ill and death is imminent.

Nancy Cruzan did not have a terminal illness. She was not protected by the Living Will laws of most states. Although she would never recover, she would, in contrast, survive for seven years in a permanent vegetative state.

The U.S. Census of 1990 gives the resident population figure as a little under 249 million people. Approximately ten thousand Americans are in a vegetative coma, like Nancy Cruzan. Individuals in this condition are so usually as the result of an accident.

A "permanent vegetative state" is the term to refer to a condition caused by a brain injury. The victim is unable to respond to their surroundings and is not aware of anything, even though the eyes may periodically open. It is similar to a coma, in that the person is unresponsive, but it is a permanent condition that a person may live in or be kept alive indefinitely either by natural or artificial means. A head injury, stroke or other events may also bring about the same resulting condition.

At the present time, the "standard" Living Will only pertains to situations involving a terminal illness. By interpretation of the law, in some states this does not include a persistent vegetative condition. The inclusion of a "terminal condition," is honored in some states. This is defined as one which is "caused by injury, disease or illness, from which to a reasonable degree of medical probability there can be no recovery and death is imminent."

There might be reluctance to honor your Living Will if the case isn't clearly within the purview of the state's Living Will law. Some state laws do say, for example, that life-support systems can be withheld only when death is imminent. However, the key is how we define imminent. One court interpretation could be to mean death will occur within hours. Therefore, this court interpretation clearly might exclude someone who could live for a number of months, a year or longer.

Some states also differ on whether or not someone can be removed from life-support systems who is in a coma. States differ in regard to whether removing a feeding tube is legally and ethically different from removing a respirator.

The varying interpretations of Living Wills from state to state result in some...

CHAPTER FOUR

BASIC QUESTIONS ABOUT THE LIVING WILL

IS IT SUFFICIENT THAT I WANT A LIVING WILL?

NO. It is not enough that you want to sign a Living Will. In order to be sure it is honored, you have to go out of your way and let your decision be known to everyone who could be involved—spouse, children, doctor, minister, attorney, and friends.

WHAT MUST YOU DO?
1. Sign the form.
2. Have it witnessed by two adults.
3. Have it notarized, if required.
4. Keep it updated according to your state law.
5. Give it to the necessary parties.
6. Have notification on your person, at all times, that you have a Living Will.

IS THERE A SPECIAL FORM FOR A LIVING WILL DOCU-MENT?

YES. Most states that have enacted Living Will statutes have model Treatment Directives. These are form documents which are fairly standardized with blanks for the person executing the Treatment Directives' to put their:
1. Name.
2. Signature and names of witnesses to the declarant's signature who should be present when the declarant signs so that they can, if required, later confirm that signature is the declarant's and comment regarding the circumstances surrounding the signing. This is

especially true if there is concern that the signing of the Treatment Directive was coerced.

3.   Address.

4.   Date of execution.

It is generally best to adhere to all Treatment Directive language as closely as possible to ascertain that it is written, signed and witnessed in accordance with the state's requirements and the model provided, to prevent later objections to the implementation of the Directive.

ARE THERE SPECIFIC INDIVIDUALS WHO SHOULD WITNESS MY LIVING WILL?

GENERALLY, YES. In order to avoid any challenges to a Living Will later, it is best to have witnesses who would have no reason to force the declarant to sign a Living Will. Therefore, it is best to exclude as witnesses any individuals:

1.   Related by blood or by marriage.
2.   Who stand to inherit by will or by law from the declarant's estate.
3.   Who would have claim against the declarant's estate.
4.   Who would be financially responsible for the declarant.
5.   Who would be named as beneficiaries of any life insurance policies that have been taken on the declarant. Often, for business reasons or as gifts for special friends, life insurance policies are taken out as a deferred means of repayment.
6.   Deemed involved with the declarant's care, as well as their employee, or any employees where the declarant may be placed for care.
7.   Employees in your attorney's or court office or any health-care provider facility who might not be readily available or have moved and not be able to be reached if the Living Will is ever challenged.

THEREFORE, FRIENDS/NEIGHBORS OF LONG STANDING ARE YOUR BEST CHOICE AS WITNESSES.

IS THERE ANYTHING I CAN DO IF I DO NOT BELIEVE THAT MY STATE'S TREATMENT DIRECTIVE DETAILS THE SPECIFICS THAT I WANT FOLLOWED?

YES. Specific, additional directions should be written as an addition to the model Treatment Directive. This way, if these instructions are deemed invalid for some reason, the directions in the model Treatment Directive are not as likely to be affected. These directions should be documented with the same formalities as the primary Treatment Directive.

IS THE AGE OF THE INDIVIDUAL TO EXECUTE A LIVING WILL UNIFORM?

NO. While most statues specify that a person must be eighteen or older to execute a Living Will, it may specify only that they be executed by a person who has reached the "age of majority or adulthood." When there is no indication in the statute as to what age defines adulthood, similar state statutes establishing the "age of majority" are used for guidance.

Individuals under twenty-one years of age, who live in states with statutes not specifying a minimum age, may wish to consult with an attorney prior to executing a Living Will. It would generally appear, however, that anyone eighteen or older would be legally authorized. There are only a small number of states which provide procedures for minors to execute a Living Will.

"Emancipated Minors" are generally qualified as persons under the age of eighteen who have established independence of their parents or guardian. They are permitted in some states to document Treatment Directives. However, in other states the statutes provide that on behalf of minors a Living Will may be documented.

MUST ONE BE COMPETENT TO MAKE A LIVING WILL?

USUALLY, YES. A statement of competency is generally included in the model Living Will statute, and many state statutes specifically so require, while others do not.

ARE THERE ANY PROVISIONS UNDER WHICH INCOM-PETENT ADULTS MAY MAKE A LIVING WILL?

YES. A list of authorized individuals in accordance with various state statutes to draft a Living Will on behalf of incompetent adults generally specifies the order in which they are authorized if those previously listed are unavailable. It seems these provisions would apply whether the person has always been incompetent, mental retardation being an example, or if they were rendered incompetent from a severe illness.

MUST ONE BE DIAGNOSED AS HAVING A TERMINAL CONDITION OR ILLNESS TO EXECUTE A LIVING WILL?

NOT ALWAYS, NO. However, some states decree a Living Will is not legally binding unless the declarant is so diagnosed. However, in most of these states, the individual can be protected. They can have any existing Living Will re-executed to give them safeguards in accord with preclusions of state statute.

MUST THERE BE CERTAIN CONDITIONS WHEREBY MY LIVING WILL COULD BE USED?

GENERALLY, YES. Most state statutes provide for the withdrawal of medical treatment when the patient has been diagnosed to be in a "terminal condition" and is not able to communicate with those around them. Most statutes only provide for withdrawal of "life-sustaining," or "life-prolong-ing," or similar types of medical treatment.

SOME STATES FORBID ENFORCEMENT OF A LIVING WILL IF THE DECLARANT IS PREGNANT.

IS THERE A TIME LIMIT ON MY LIVING WILL, AND MUST I DO ANYTHING TO KEEP IT CURRENT?

GENERALLY, NO. Unless the declarant revokes his or her Living Will, it generally remains in effect throughout the declarant's lifetime, once executed. However, since some states do require that it be re-executed on a periodic basis, it is best for everyone who cares enough to make a Living Will in the first place to give an annual review of his or her Living Will as a part of routine personal medical hygiene. It would be best to sign and date it again every two years. Then, every five years, take your Living Will out to sign and have witnessed and also have notarized, if required by state statute.

The overruling reason to review and revise your Living Will in accordance with advances in medical treatment and technology is that by keeping it current, your advance directive is more likely to be upheld in court should question of its implementation ever have to be legally determined.

WHAT IF I HAVE A LIVING WILL AND WANT TO CHANGE MY MIND, CAN I?
      YES.

IF I HAVE DEFINITELY DECIDED I NO LONGER WANT MY LIVING WILL IN EFFECT, WHAT SHOULD I DO?

Methods of revocation are generally broad and take place upon any expression by the declarant that their intent is that their Living Will no longer be in effect. However, some states do require the revocation be not just oral. They require the Living Will be not only witnessed by non-involved parties, but that it must be documented, signed by the declarant and witnessed, in order to be revoked.

WHO ARE THE NECESSARY PARTIES TO BE GIVEN A COPY OF MY LIVING WILL?

1. Your designated individual Durable Power of Attorney for Health Care.
2. Your physician, who should make it part of your permanent medical records. MAKE CERTAIN TO TRANSFER IT WITH YOUR RECORDS IF YOU MOVE OR CHANGE DOCTORS.
3. Your clergyman.
4. Your attorney.
5. Your neighbor.
6. Your local hospital.

The human body, that Living Wills strive to protect, is indeed a unique creation that has tremendous capacity and adaptability directed by enormous intelligence. The engine of this creation is the human heart. It beats about one hundred thousand times every twenty-four hours, and pumps about six quarts of blood through over ninety-six thousand miles of blood vessels. This amounts to sixty-three hundred gallons pumped per day, working constantly without missing a beat year after year. And, we have only directed attention to one of the body's systems, the circulatory system.

If our circulatory system is working at full capacity and blood is going to our brain, then our decision to complete a Living Will is a personal one that needs knowledge of individual state statutes, state by state.

WHAT SHOULD I DO IF MY HOME STATE DOESN'T HAVE A STANDARD LIVING WILL DOCUMENT?

If you reside in a state without a Living Will law, you can still protect your health-care rights by signing a standard Living Will document, as given on the next page, until there is a state statute where you live.

While the required form of a "Living Will" may vary from state to state, a properly executed "Living Will" should be easily enforceable in the state in which it is drafted. And these statutes under the Living Will do offer significant legal protections.

One protection is that those who would be involved in the cessation of medical treatment are generally immunized by statute from any liability for permitting the patient to die. Furthermore, having their rights of legal prosecution protected, the medical staff and those individuals concerned with the patient's well-being can not only interact better on their own behalf, but also can interact better to aid the patient, for whom all have a common sick-bed concern.

Another legal protection provided those having a "Living Will" that is of significant importance is that when put into effect, life insurance benefits are generally paid. Some individuals might be worried that these benefits would be jeopardized by termination of medical treatment. Nearly all Living Will laws clearly state that new life insurance applications cannot be turned down, nor can existing policies be cancelled.

Individuals who want to complete a Living Will, but do not have any state statute where they reside, often want to make their own arrangements. The Advance Directive-Living Will that follows is provided by the Lakeland Regional Medical

Center, Incorporated, as the result of an LRMC multi-disciplinary effort to provide a community service.

Appointment of a Health Care Surrogate:

Now that you have made your wishes known, you may choose a person to make medical decisions which may not have been specifically addressed by your ADVANCE DIRECTIVE-LIVING WILL. This person is called your HEALTH CARE SURROGATE and if you are unable to make your own decisions, he/she will have the authority to:

(a) Act for you to make health care decisions which he/she believes you would have made under the circumstances if you were able;

(b) Consult with appropriate health care providers to provide informed consent in your best interest and give consent in writing on the appropriate forms;

(c) Have access to your clinical records and authority to release information and clinical records to appropriate persons to provide continuity of care;

(d) Apply for public benefits (such as Medicare and Medicaid) for you and have access to information about your income and assets as needed to make the application; and

(e) Authorize the transfer and/or admission of you to or from a health care facility.

I hereby execute this ADVANCE DIRECTIVE-LIVING WILL and appoint _____(enter none if Surrogate is not being appointed) as my Health Care Surrogate and authorize him/her to make all decisions for me which he/she believes I would have made.

As to decisions regarding the withholding or withdrawing of life-prolonging procedures (including artificial nutrition and hydration):

_____I DO AUTHORIZE my surrogate to make such decisions.

_____I DO NOT AUTHORIZE my surrogate to make such decisions.

I understand the full import of this declaration, and I am emotionally and mentally competent to make this declaration.

_____   _____
(Date)   (Declarant's Signature)

The declarant is known to me, and I believe him or her to be of sound mind.

_____   _____
(Date)   (Witness - any adult)

(Witness - cannot be spouse, blood relative, heir or person responsible for health care costs)

I hereby accept the above designation as Health Care Surrogate:

_____   _____
(Date)   (Signature of Surrogate - can be signed

at any time prior to acting as surrogate)

ARE LIVING WILLS FILLED OUT IN ACCORDANCE WITH ONE STATE STATUTE HONORED IF YOU ARE HOSPITALIZED IN A DIFFERENT STATE?

This important question does not have a uniform answer. According to Congressional Research Service (CRS) Report for Congress on Treatment and Appointment

Directives, dated 1/14/91:

"4.   PORTABILITY OF MEDICAL DIRECTIVES

Concerns have been raised that a living will or other Directive executed in one state might not be honored in another state. Some states have specifically provided that a Directive executed in another state is valid in the subject state. However, even if one state has not specifically provided for the enforcement of Directives from another state, a person's constitutional rights are not effected by moving within the United States. Assuming that an individual had clearly set out his or her wishes with sufficient detail to cover a particular medical situation, and that it was completed with sufficient formality, it would appear that any state court would be required to acknowledge the document, and give effect to it. Absent some indication of fraud or changed circumstance, the imposition of specific technical requirements such as the form or number of witnesses would appear to be inconsistent with an individual's constitutional right to refuse medical treatment."

Yet, according to the Department of Health and Human Services, in "Summary of Federal Statute Concerning Advance Directives":

"The law on honoring advance directives from another state is unclear. Because an advance directive tells your wishes regarding medical care, it may be honored wherever you are, if it is made known. *But, if you spend a great deal of time in one state you may wish to consider having your Advance Directive meet the laws of both states, as much as possible."*

It seems we have great need to have our "papers" in order—signed, sealed, witnessed, and ready for expeditious delivery to whatever facility we have been admitted. Most important it seems is the need to address and correct the issue for one standardized Living Will and Durable Power of Attorney for Health Care document.

Since the 1950s, most patients spend their final days, which often stretch into months or years, in medical facilities. They are attached, more often than not, to highly sophisticated technical equipment that has the ability to continue their lives with only the thinnest thread holding them to the needle's eye of this world.

Two old cliches meet, bringing needles and pins and dollars and cents together, so that both sides of the scales for individual justice come into balance with everyone having signed advance directives.

On one side of the scale we have Living Wills, and on the other we need to have...

CHAPTER FIVE

DURABLE POWER OF ATTORNEY FOR HEALTH CARE (DPAHC)

Having a "Living Will" is only the movement of one foot in the momentous advancement of the second foot to complete one giant step. In order to ensure that your medical wishes are carried out as you have outlined in advance of the time when need has presented itself that you might be deemed incompetent, the document used to designate your medical decision-making power is called a Durable Power of Attorney for Health Care (DPAHC).

While some Living Wills may appoint a health proxy, it is important to understand their scope of authority and that of a power of attorney. As with the power of attorney, the health proxy may be given specific instructions by the declarant regarding medical treatment they would want provided, or that the proxy may be given discretion in this decision.

However, the significant difference between these two appointments and that of a designated individual as your Durable Power of Attorney for Health Care agent is that they can only be exercised when a patient is terminally ill.

A healthy proxy or individual given your "power of attorney" would not be able to render decisions on your behalf if you were in a variety of "other" health conditions. For example, if you had advanced Alzheimer's disease, or were in a coma like Nancy Cruzan, your medical proxy could not act alone on your behalf to see that your wishes were followed.

The more inclusive document for everyone to have, in addition to a Living Will, is a DPAHC document. This permits your agent to act for you in most health-care matters, including those you might not have considered.

Many American citizens will find themselves in life-altering situations in medical facilities, without the luxury of forethought for decision making that gift wraps elective health-care procedures versus emergency treatment. At the time of emergency treatment, it may very likely not be possible for people to complete an advance directive. Therefore it is imperative to have both documents in advance of the time for their actual use.

Your Durable Power of Attorney has the right to manage your money and make your health decisions. But, he or she is not liable for the costs of your health care, even though able to authorize medical care.

A person who uses this document does not have to plan for all of the varying medical situations that may arise. It is by having given someone this responsibility that medical treatment decisions can be deferred until such time as the situation has climaxed. As a result, the decision maker can evaluate the specific details of the medical situation as they develop, before a conclusion is reached.

The person you appoint as your DPAHC agent need not be an attorney. In fact, while bankers and lawyers frequently serve as attorney-in-fact for other business, your health-care decisions require that someone have personal knowledge of you, so that they can make the decision you would want.

Your designated Durable Power of Attorney for Health Care agent can be given to any competent adult, with some exceptions, whether they be family, friend or other, who can weigh the specific circumstances of the situation and the choices available, and make a decision. However, a close family member may not always be the best choice as your DPAHC agent, because he or she may be hesitant to invoke a patient's wishes for terminating care. In fact, surveys suggest that many are more reluctant to terminate a relative's life-sustaining care than they would be to put into effect a cease-and-desist order for their own treatment. The reason is: having to bear the lifelong emotional responsibility for verbalizing the decision that took "Grand-Dad" to heaven.

According to a 1990 Gallup Poll, most Americans—84%—say that if they were on life-support systems and had no hope of recovering, they would want treatment withheld. Yet, being able to say "turn that off," when it means the end of life to one you love, is not the equivalent of the parental order as it pertains to the stereo. Indeed, surrogates can become so overwhelmed by grief or responsibility, they are unable to carry out a DPAHC document.

The social contract between doctors and patients is to sustain life and relieve suffering. But there are times when these ideals are in conflict and laws must be abided. A wisely-appointed individual as your Durable Power of Attorney for Health Care agent helps when this occurs.

Furthermore, it may be advisable that two DPAHC are named to act for you. This is critical in case one may not be immediately reached when critical decisions have to be made. Either one should be able to act alone to avoid inaction or delay. Obviously, this means that both appointees must be of like and unwavering mind, in accordance with your desires.

The choice of the word "durable" to qualify the individual given another's Power of Health Care is most appropriate. *Webster's Dictionary* defines durable as: "having the quality of being not perishable or changeable." This is a vital qualification of the power one is entrusting to another individual on their behalf. It becomes as the flower of friendship and marriage that survives tumultuous upheavals, because each has nurtured the other to withstand life's storms. So the love continues to bloom within the one remaining, even beyond the demise of the other half. Each had so fully complemented the other that there was no longer top or bottom, flower or stem, to the extent that the only thing to do is to continue as the solo reflection of what is past.

While belief is not ours to question, there are.....

CHAPTER SIX

ROUTINE QUESTIONS REGARDING A DURABLE POWER OF ATTORNEY FOR HEALTH CARE

Hopefully, the following selected ones and given answers will fulfill the needs of most individuals:

IS IT SUFFICIENT THAT I WANT TO DESIGNATE A DPAHC AGENT?
NO. Your DPAHC and designated agent must be documented, because while state statutes vary, the only legal justification for implementation of your desires, should they be challenged, is to have a properly documented DPAHC.

Certain States specifically provide that the power to make decisions regarding life-sustaining treatments may be transferred. Yet other states give permission for the appointment of a power of attorney for all purposes, and still they give no direction as to whether or not this appointment would be authorized in medically-related matters. In these cases, interpretation by the courts of that state gives the ultimate authorization for decisions when legally challenged. And a few states specifically restrict the use of statutes for these purposes.

IS THERE A SPECIAL FORM?
SOMETIMES, YES. However, only a few of the states that have enacted statutes covering Appointment Directives provide DPAHC model documents. As with Living Wills, states vary so regarding whether a document may be used if it is not the same as the model. If one is provided, it is best to adhere as closely as possible and to all formalities to prevent later objections.

SHOULD MY DPAHC DOCUMENT BE WITNESSED, AND IF SO, BY ANY PARTICULAR INDIVIDUALS?

GENERALLY, YES. Since most states require two adult witnesses or a notary sign a DPAHC document, it is best to do both and follow the same selection qualifications for witnesses given for your Living Will.

WHAT IS THE SCOPE OF AUTHORITY OF MY DPAHC AGENT?

While the DPAHC scope of authority is generally established by the document's terms, it may also be dictated by state statute. For example: A state, while allowing the DPAHC agent to enforce the document, does not give him or her independent decision powers.

Therefore, it seems generally that the same legal restraints for withdrawal of health care to be implemented with a Living Will are to be used in curtailing the use of inappropriately defined life-supportive measures.

Health-care providers may be less likely to comply with a non-statutory directive. Therefore, they will more probably comply when one is followed. It is likely that a court order could be obtained to require compliance with the authority the declarant trusted, if necessary.

IS THE AGE OF THE INDIVIDUAL APPOINTING A DPAHC UNIFORM?

GENERALLY, NO. Unlike Living Will statutes, very few covering DPAHC specify at what age an individual may make this appointment in their behalf. However, a child who, by legal definition specified by age, could not generally make this designation. This is because most statutes say the power is limited to the standard legal powers of the declarant. Clearly this would not be considered appropriate for a child to determine.

MUST ONE BE COMPETENT TO APPOINT A DURABLE POWER OF ATTORNEY FOR HEALTH CARE?

GENERALLY, YES. However, states that do not in their statutes so specify, sometimes include a statement of competency within their model DPAHC document.

SHOULD DOCUMENTATION OF MY APPOINTED DPAHC BE UPDATED?

GENERALLY, NO. It is not necessary, but, as with Living Wills, it is good to do so as a part of routine good medical hygiene.

WHAT SHOULD I DO WITH MY DPAHC DOCUMENT?

Put it in a safe, fireproof place, where it is easily accessible if it is needed. DO NOT KEEP IT IN A SAFE-DEPOSIT BOX.

Many people keep a small card in their purse or wallet (often with their driver's license) which states that:

1. They have a DPAHC document.
2. Where signed copies are located.
3. They have named DPAHC, and how to contact them.

WILL MY DPAHC DOCUMENT BE HONORED IF I AM IN CRITICAL CONDITION IN A STATE DIFFERENT THAN THE STATE STATUTE I FOLLOWED?

GENERALLY, YES. A few states have specifically provided that such documents are valid in their states, although executed in another. Moreover, if a state has not put enforcement limitations of Advance Directives documented in accord with statutes of another state, the directives should not be affected.

Rights of the individual should not be threatened by virtue of the fact that they are exercising their right of mobility within and beyond the United States.

The following three conditional situations are frequently the categorical divisions that need a declarant to have reviewed with his or her designated DPAHC:

1. A coma or a persistent vegetative state, with hope of recovery, or to become aware of one's surroundings, or to be able to use one's mental abilities;
2. A progressive illness, which will continue to worsen and result in death, and which cannot be improved or cured;
3. A condition which makes one unable to recognize people or speak understandably, and the

condition is permanent and cannot be improved cured, but is *not* terminal;

The questions that follow provide for these conditions and were drafted by the Lakeland Regional Medical Center, Incorporated as the result of an LRMC multi-disciplinary effort to provide community service.

INSTRUCTIONS FOR COMPLETION: If you were in the condition described in the three situations, what would your choice be regarding the possible treatments listed? Make your choice by placing your initials in the appropriate space.

NOTE: In many cases in the situations described below, it may take days or even weeks for the prognosis to be established. In the interim, until the outlook is known, some of the treatments listed may be appropriate. Only after the prognosis is known with reasonable medical certainty is it appropriate to withdraw or withhold such treatments.

The situations described assume your physician and at least two consultants share the opinion regarding the outlook for your recovery. The possible treatments are considered only if medically reasonable.

POSSIBLE TREATMENTS: Assume none of the following will improve or cure the condition described in the situations:

1.   Do you want efforts to be made to resuscitate (chest massage, artificial breathing) you if your heart or breathing stop?

2.   If you are unable to breathe on your own, do you want a mechanical breathing machine to be used?

3.   If your kidneys fail, do you want kidney dialysis (cleaning the blood through a machine) even if it cannot improve or cure your condition?

4.   Do you want any surgery, even if it is life-saving, if it cannot improve or cure your condition?

5.   Do you want pain medications to keep you comfortable even if they dull consciousness and could shorten your life?

6.   Do you want other medications, such as antibiotics, which may prolong your life?

7.   Do you want food and water given to you

through tubes in your veins, nose or stomach?

8.   Other: _____

Situation A
If I am in a coma, or in what is called a persistent vegetative state, and have no hope of recovery or of becoming aware of my surroundings or being able to use my mental abilities, then my wishes regarding the following would be:

(In answer to questions 1. through 8.)

_____Yes   _____No _____Undecided

Situation B
If I have a progressive illness, which will continue to worsen and result in my death and which cannot be improved or cured, when the point is reached that I am no longer able to recognize family and friends or speak understandabley, my wishes regarding the following would be:

(In answer to questions 1. through 8.)

_____Yes   _____No _____Undecided

Situation C
If I have a condition which makes me unable to recognize people or speak understandably, and that condition is permanent and cannot be imporived or cured but is NOT terminal, my wishes regarding the following would be:

(In answer to questions 1. through 8.)

_____Yes   _____No _____Undecided

It is hoped that people will see their Living Will and DPAHC documents as vehicles to ensure that their death will not be prolonged when the time to implement them has arrived. It is by designating someone as your DPAHC that you may avoid the added tragedy of deathbed fights that can occur among the patient's loved ones when all have mutually-shared concerns, but different perspectives of the prognosis and their own consciences.

The loving wife of many years, who has witnessed the degenerating health of her husband for several years, may say, "I want to do what he and I would feel is best for him." An equally loving daughter or son might say, "I'm not going to let you kill my father."

The appointment of an individual outside the family circle as the designated Durable Power of Attorney for Health Care agent may not erase the possibility altogether of an emotional conflict of opinions. However, regardless of whom you designate, doing so will eliminate the fight for control and barrage of legal sheets crisscrossing what needs to be, for the

If you do become incapacitated, the durable power of attorney stays in force *only* during this period. When you are able to speak for yourself, no one has the right to speak for you. *Only* during your incapacity can the decision-making powers in either document—the Living Will and the DPAHC—be used.

The following Appointment Directives are examples from the selected states of Kentucky, Texas, and West Virginia.

KENTUCKY—APPOINTMENT DIRECTIVE
DESIGNATION OF HEALTH CARE SURROGATE

I designate _____ as my health care surrogate(s) to make any health care decisions for me when I no longer have decisional capacity.

If _____ refuses or is not able to act for me, I designate _____ as my health care surrogate(s).

Any prior designation is revoked.

Signed this ____ day of _____, 19__.

Signature and address of the grantor.

In our joint presence, the grantor, who is of sound mind and eighteen years of age, or older, voluntarily dated and signed this writing or directed it to be dated and signed for the grantor.

Signature and address of witness.

Signature and address of witness.

STATE OF KENTUCKY

_____ County

Before me, the undersigned authority, came the grantor who is of sound mind and eighteen (18) years of age, or older, and acknowledged that he voluntarily dated and signed this writing or directed it to be signed and dated as above.

Done this ____ day of _____, 19__.

_____
Signature of Notary Public or other officer

Date commission expires: _____

(Enact. Acts 1990, ch. 123 § 7, effective July 13, 1990.)

TEXAS—APPOINTMENT DIRECTIVE

INFORMATION CONCERNING THE DURABLE POWER OF ATTORNEY FOR HEALTH CARE

THIS IS AN IMPORTANT LEGAL DOCUMENT. BEFORE SIGNING THIS DOCUMENT, YOU SHOULD KNOW THESE IMPORTANT FACTS:

Except to the extent you state otherwise, this document gives the person you name as your agent the authority to make any and all health care decisions for you in accordance with your wishes, including your religious and moral beliefs, when you are no longer capable of making them yourself. Because "health care" means any treatment, service, or procedure to maintain, diagnose, or treat your physical or mental condition, your agent has the power to make a broad range of health care decisions for you. Your agent may consent, refuse to consent, or withdraw consent to medical treatment and may make decisions about withdrawing or withholding life-sustaining treatment. Your agent may not consent to voluntary inpatient mental health services, convulsive treatment, psychosurgery, or abortion. A physician must comply with your agent's instructions or allow you to be transferred to another physician.

Your agent's authority begins when your doctor certifies that you lack the capacity to make health care decisions.

Your agent is obligated to follow your instructions when making decisions on your behalf. Unless you state otherwise, your agent has the same authority to make decisions about your health care as you would have had.

It is important that you discuss this document with your physician or other health care provider before you sign it to make sure that you understand the nature and range of decisions that may be made on your behalf. If you do not have a physician, you should talk with someone else who is knowledgeable about these issues and can answer your questions. You do not need a lawyer's assistance to complete this document, but if there is anything in this document that you do not understand, you should ask a lawyer to explain it to you.

The person you appoint as agent should be someone you know and trust. The person must be 18 years of age or older or a person under 18 years of age who has had the disabilities of minority removed. If you appoint your health or residential care provider (e.g., your physician or an employee of a home health agency, hospital, nursing home, or residential care home, other than a relative), that person has to choose between acting as your agent or as your health or residential care provider; the law does not permit a person to do both at the same time.

You should inform the person you appoint that you want the person to be your health care agent. You should discuss this document with your agent and your physician and give each a signed copy. You should indicate on the document itself the people and institutions who have signed copies. Your agent is not liable for health care decisions made in good faith on your behalf.

Even after you have signed this document, you have the right to make health care decisions for yourself as long as you are able to do so and treatment cannot be given to you or stopped over your objection. You have the right to revoke the authority granted to your agent by informing your agent or your health or residential care provider orally or in writing, or by your execution of a subsequent durable power of attorney for health care. Unless you state otherwise, your appointment of a spouse dissolves on divorce.

This document may not be changed or modified. If you want to make changes in the document, you must make an entirely new one.

You may wish to designate an alternate agent in the event that your agent is unwilling, unable, or ineligible to act as your agent. Any alternate agent your designate has the same authority to make health care decisions for you.

THIS POWER OF ATTORNEY IS NOT VALID UNLESS IT IS SIGNED IN THE PRESENCE OF TWO OR MORE QUALIFIED WITNESSES. THE FOLLOWING PERSONS MAY NOT ACT AS WITNESSES:

(1) the person you have designated as your agent;

(2) your health or residential care provider or an employee of your health or residential care provider;

(3) your spouse;

(4) your lawful heirs or beneficiaries named in your will or a deed; or

(5) creditors or persons who have a claim against you.
Durable power of attorney form

Sec. 16. The durable power of attorney for health care must be in substantially the following form:

DURABLE POWER OF ATTORNEY FOR HEALTH CARE DESIGNATION OF HEALTH CARE AGENT.

    I,_____ (insert your name) appoint:
    Name: _____
    Address: _____
    _____ Phone _____

as my agent to make any and all health care decisions for me, except to the extent I state otherwise in this document. This durable power of attorney for health care takes effect if I become unable to make my own health care decisions and this fact is certified in writing by my physician.

DESIGNATION OF ALTERNATE AGENT.

(You are not required to designate an alternate agent but you may do so. An alternate agent may make the same health care decision as the designated agent if the designated agent is unable or unwilling to act as your agent. If the agent designated is your spouse, the designation is automatically revoked by law if your marriage is dissolved.)

If the person designated as my agent is unable or unwilling to make health care decisions for me, I designate the following persons to serve as my agent to make health care decisions for me as authorized by this document, who serve in the following order:

A. *First Alternate Agent*

    Name: _____
    Address: _____
    _____ Phone _____

B. Second Alternate Agent

    Name: _____
    Address: _____
    _____ Phone _____

The original of this document is kept at _____
_____

The following individuals or institutions have signed copies:

Name: _____

Address: _____

_____

Name: _____

Address: _____

_____

DURATION.

    I understand that this power of attorney exists indefinitely from the date I execute this document unless I establish a shorter time or revoke the power of attorney. If I am unable to make health care decisions for myself when this power of attorney expires, the authority I have granted my agent continues to exist until the time I become able to make health care decisions for myself.

    (IF APPLICABLE) This power of attorney ends on the following date: _____

PRIOR DESIGNATIONS REVOKED.

    I revoke any prior durable power of attorney for health care.

ACKNOWLEDGEMENT OF DISCLOSURE STATEMENT.

    I have been provided with a disclosure statement explaining the effect of this document. I have read and understand that information contained in the disclosure statement.

    (YOU MUST DATE AND SIGN THIS POWER OF ATTORNEY)

    I sign my name to this durable power of attorney for health care on ___ day of _____ 19__ at (City and State)

        (Signature) _____

        (Print Name) _____

STATEMENT OF WITNESSES.

    I declare under penalty of perjury that the principal has identified himself or herself to me, that the principal signed or acknowledged this durable power of attorney in my presence, that I believe the principal to be of sound mind, that the principal has affirmed that the principal is aware of the nature of the document and is signing it voluntarily and free from duress, that the principal requested that I serve as witness to the principal's execution of this document, that I am not the person appointed as agent by this document, and that I am not a provider of health or residential care, an employee of a provider of health or residential care, the operator of a community care facility, or an employee of an operator of a health care facility.

    I declare that I am not related to the principal by blood, marriage, or adoption and that to the best of my knowledge I am not entitled to any part of the estate of the principal on the death of the principal under a will or by operation of law.

    Witness Signature: _____

    Print Name: _____ Date _____

    Address: _____

Witness Signature: _____
Print Name: _____ Date _____
Address: _____

* WEST VIRGINIA - APPOINTMENT DIRECTIVE *
MEDICAL POWER OF ATTORNEY
Dated: _____, 19 ____.

    I,_____,(insert your name and address), hereby appoint _____ (insert the name, address, area code and telephone number of the person you wish to designate as your representative) as my representative to act on my behalf to give, withhold or withdraw in formed consent to health care decisions in the event that I am not able to do so myself. If my representative is unable, unwilling or disqualified to serve, then I appoint _____ as my successor representative.

    This appointment shall extend to (but not be limited to) decisions relating to medical treatment, surgical treatment, nursing care, medication, hospitalization, care and treatment in a nursing home or other facility, and home health care. The representative appointed by this document is specifically authorized to act on my behalf to consent to, refuse or withdraw any and all medical treatment or diagnostic procedures, if my representative determines that I, if able to do so, would consent to, refuse or withdraw such treatment or procedures. Such authority shall include, but not be limited to, the withholding or withdrawal of life-prolonging intervention when in the opinion of two physicians who have examined me, one of whom is my attending physician, such life-prolonging intervention offers no medical hope of benefit.

    I appoint this representative because I believe this person understands my wishes and values and will act to carry into effect the health care decisions that I would make if I were able to do so, and because I also believe that this person will act in my best interest when my wishes are unknown. It is my intent that my family, my physician and all legal authorities be bound by the decisions that are made by the representative appointed by this document, and it is my intent that these decisions should not be the subject of review by any health care provider, or administrative or judicial agency.

    It is my intent that this document be legally binding and effective. In the event that the law does not recognize this document as legally binding and effective, it is my intent that this document be taken as a formal statement of my desire concerning the method by which any health care decisions should be made on my behalf during any period when I am unable to make such decisions.

    In exercising the authority under this medical power of attorney, my representative shall act consistently with my special directives or limitations as stated below.

    SPECIAL DIRECTIVES OR LIMITATIONS ON THIS POWER: (If none, write "none.")

_____
_____

THIS MEDICAL POWER OF ATTORNEY SHALL BECOME EF-
FECTIVE ONLY UPON MY INCAPACITY TO GIVE, WITHHOLD OR
WITHDRAW INFORMED CONSENT TO MY OWN MEDICAL CARE.

These directives shall supersede any directives made in any
previously executed document concerning my health care.

X _____

Signature of Principal

I did not sign the principal's signature above. I am at least
eighteen years of age and am not related to the principal by blood or
marriage. I am not entitled to any portion of the estate of the principal
according to the laws of intestate succession of the state of the principal's
domicile or to the best of my knowledge under any will of the principal
or codicil thereto, or legally responsible for the costs of the principal's
medical or other care. I am not the principal's attending physician, nor
am I the representative or successor representative of the principal.

WITNESS:DATE:

_____   _____

WITNESS:DATE:

_____   _____

STATE OF _____,
COUNTY OF _____, to-wit:

I, _____, a Notary Public of said County, do
certify that _____, as principal, and
_____ and _____, as witnesses, whose names are
signed to the writing above bearing date on the ___ day of _____, 19
__, have this day acknowledged the same before.

Given under my hand this ___ day of _____, 19 __.

My commission expires: _____

_____

Notary Public

The proper execution of Advance Directives guards
against any legal resistance to implementation of them. State
statute varies in regard to:

1.   Specific requirements;
2.   Whether or not model forms have been adopted;
3.   Whether or not additional provisions may be outlined;
4.   Witness specifications;
5.   Need of notarization; and
6.   Term of expiration, if any.

As safeguard against further disaster when facing a life-death crisis, and the time has arrived to put into effect one's Living Will/Treatment Directive and/or Durable Power of Attorney for Health Care Document/Appointment Directive, the careful compliance of instructions dictated by each state is mandatory. These requirements are in varying detail, according to...

CHAPTER SEVEN

STATE REQUIREMENTS FOR EXECUTION OF ADVANCE DIRECTIVES

ALABAMA

1. Provides a model Living Will/Treatment Directive.

2. Living Will prepared "should be" substantially the same.

3. States that more specific directions may be included.

4. Person must be an adult to execute a Living Will, but there is no indication in the statute as to what age qualifies.

5. Persons making the Living Will must be "of sound mind," and this must be confirmed by two witnesses who sign and:

    a) are 19 years old or older;

    b) may not have signed Living Will on behalf of or direction of declarant;

    c) may not be related to declarant by blood or marriage;

    d) may not be eligible to inherit from declarant's estate;

    e) may not be directly responsible for the declarant's care.

6. Law provides a Living Will only allows withdrawal of medical treatment when:

    a) diagnosis states declarant "terminally ill";

    b) diagnosis states declarant "terminally ill or injured";

    c) diagnosis states declarant's "death is imminent";

    d) diagnosis states declarant's condition is "hopeless."

7. Law says those medical procedures which can be withdrawn are "those which would serve only to prolong

the dying process and which ultimately would not prevent the death from occurring."

8. Living Will is not to be in effect during a declarant's pregnancy.

9. THERE IS CASE LAW SUPPORTING NON-STATU-TORY DIRECTIVE WHICH WOULD ALLOW MEDICAL TREATMENT TO BE TERMINATED WITHOUT A WRITTEN DIRECTIVE.

ALASKA

1. Provides a model Living Will/Treatment Directive.

2. Living Will prepared "may, but need not," follow the model.

3. Declaration executed in another state which complies with law of that state will be honored by State of Alaska.

4. Person who is at least eighteen may execute a Living Will.

5. Person making a Living Will must be "competent."

6. Living Will must be signed by two witnesses who must:

> a) be at least eighteen years of age;
> b) not be related to declarant by blood or marriage;
> c) not be a state official "such as a judge or a notary public."

7. Law provides a Living Will only allows withdrawal of medical treatment when:

> a) diagnosis states declarant is in a "terminal condition";
> b) diagnosis states declarant's "death must be expected to occur within a relatively short time."

8. Law says those medical procedures which can be withdrawn are "those which would only prolong the dying process.

9. Living Will is not to be in effect during pregnancy.

10. Provides a "Statutory Form Power of Attorney Act."

11. Provides a model form, and gives declarant option to make Power of Attorney effective even if they become disabled. One of the optional powers given the appointed individual is power to make health-care services decisions, but may not authorize withdrawal of life-sustaining procedures. However, the Act does give the decision maker the authority to endeavor to enforce a Living Will under the Alaska Rights of the Terminally Ill Act.

12. There is no case law supporting non-statutory directives.

ARIZONA

1. Provides a model Living Will/Treatment Directive.

2. Living Will prepared "should be" substantially the same.

3. States that more specific directions may be included.

4. Person must be an adult to execute a Living Will, and the definition of a "qualified patient" is restricted to persons eighteen years of age and older.

5. Persons making the Living Will must be "of sound mind," and this must be confirmed by two witnesses, who must sign and:

    a) be eighteen years of age or older;
    b) not be related to the declarant by blood or marriage;
    c) not be eligible to inherit from declarant;
    d) not be financially responsible for declarant;
    e) not have a claim against declarant's estate.

6. Law provides a Living Will only allows withdrawal of medical treatment when:

    a) diagnosis states declarant is in a "terminal condition";
    b) diagnosis states declarant's condition is "incurable";
    c) diagnosis states declarant's condition is "irreversible."

7. Law says those medical procedures which can be withdrawn are "those which would only prolong the dying process." It specifies that *medication, food or fluids, however, may not be withdrawn.*

8. Law provides that a Living Will is not to be in effect during a declarant's pregnancy.

9. Provides a "Powers of Attorney Act."

10. Does not provide a model form, but does provide that:

    a) on it appear that the "power of attorney shall

    not be affected by disability of the principal."
    b) The Act does not specify appointed decision maker may direct withdrawal of medical procedures.
    11. There is case law supporting non-statutory directives.

ARKANSAS

1. Provides a model Living Will/Treatment Directive.

2. Living Will prepared "may, but need not," follow the model.

3. Declarations executed in another state which comply with law of that state will be honored by State of Arkansas.

4. Person who is at least eighteen may execute a Living Will.

5. Person making the Living Will must be "of sound mind," and this must be confirmed by two witnesses at least eighteen years old, but no other specifications are given.

6. Living Will can be prepared for:

    a) a minor;

    b) a patient who is not able to make health care crisis decisions, by the following individuals, with the restriction that a person later on the list can only make a decision if the individuals preceding them are not available:

1) legal guardians of the patient, if one has been appointed;

2) parents of an unmarried patient under 18;

3) spouse of a married patient;

4) adult child of a patient or, if more than one child, the decision of the majority of the patient's adult children participating;

5) parents of a patient over the age of 18;

6) patient's adult sibling or, if more than one, a majority of the patient's adult siblings participating;

7) persons standing *in loco parentis* to the patient;

8) majority of the patient's adult heirs at law who participate.

7. Law provides a Living Will only allows withdrawal of medical treatment when:

    a) diagnosis states declarant in a "terminal condition";

    b) diagnosis states declarant's condition is "incurable";

    c) diagnosis states "death is expected to occur in a relatively short time";

d) declarant is "permanently unconscious."

8. Law says those medical procedures which can be withdrawn are "those which would only prolong the dying process, or would maintain the patient in a state of permanent unconsciousness."

9. Living Will is not to be in effect during a declarant's pregnancy.

10. Law provides for a health-care proxy, and directs the proxy's instructions to be followed.

11. There is no case law supporting non-statutory directives.

CALIFORNIA

1. Provides a model Living Will/Treatment Directive.

2. Living Will prepared "must use" model provided.

3. Person must be an adult to execute a Living Will, but there is no indication in the statute as to what age qualifies.

4. Persons making the Living Will must be "of sound mind," and this must be confirmed by two witnesses who must sign and:

> a) may not be related to declarant by blood or marriage;
> b) are not eligible to inherit from declarant;
> c) are not financially responsible for declarant's medical expenses;
> d) do not have a claim against declarant's estate;
> e) are not declarant's attending physician, or declarant's employee;
> f) are not an employee of a health facility.

5. If the person making the Living Will is in a specified category of nursing facility, one of the witnesses must be a patient advocate or ombudsman designated by the California State Department of Aging for this purpose.

6. If the person making the Living Will is in a nursing home, an administrator of the facility or an attorney should be contacted.

7. Law provides a Living Will only allows withdrawal of medical treatment when:

> a) diagnosis states declarant in a "terminal condition";
> b) diagnosis must state declarant's condition "incurable," and that "death would occur regardless of the use of medical treatment."

8. Law says those medical procedures which can be withdrawn are "those which would only prolong the dying process; and death must be imminent."

9. Law provides that a Living Will "shall be effective for five years from the date of execution."

10. The "California Statutory Form Durable Power of Attorney for Health Care Act" that specifically

provides for an Appointed Director entitled a Durable Power of Attorney for Health Care.

11. Provides a model form which should be followed and notarized by a notary public, and signed by two witnesses:

- a) who may not include a health-care provider;
- b) who may not be employees of the health care provider;
- c) who may not be the appointed decision maker;
- d) who may not be the employees or operator of a community care or residential care facility;
- e) who at least one witness may not be related by blood or marriage, or entitled to inherit from declarant.

12. Law specifies an Appointment Directive for declarant who is in a skilled-nursing facility must be signed by a patient advocate or ombudsman.

13. Law forbids the appointment of power of attorney to:

- a) health care providers who provide treatment to a declarant;
- b) any employees of the health care provider of the declarant;
- c) any employees of residential or community care facilities, with an exception made if such person is a relative by blood or marriage;
- d) conservators of the declarant.

14. Law provides a Durable Power of Attorney is valid for seven years, unless the declarant has become incompetent.

15. There is case law supporting non-statutory directives.

COLORADO

1. Provides a model Living Will/Treatment Directive.

2. Living Will prepared "may, but need not," follow the model.

3. States any adult may execute a Living Will, and defines an adult as an individual at least eighteen years of age.

4. Statute requires the person making the Living Will must be "competent."

5. Requires that the Living Will be signed by two witnesses, who are:

    a) not related to the declarant;

    b) not the declarant's attending physician;

    c) not an employee of the declarant's attending physician;

    d) not an employee of a health-care facility housing the declarant;

    e) not claimants against the declarant's estate.

6. Law provides a Living Will only allows the withdrawal of medical treatment when:

    a) diagnosis states declarant is in a "terminal condition";

    b) diagnosis states declarant's condition is "incurable";

    c) diagnosis states declarant's condition is "irreversible";

7. Law says those medical procedures which can be withdrawn are "those which would only prolong the dying process." *Nutrition and hydration can be withdrawn if an individual is in a terminal condition and is unconscious for over seven days.*

8. Living Will is not to be in effect during a declarant's pregnancy.

9. Provides a "Powers of Attorney Act."

10. Does not provide a model form, but does provide that:

    a) "this power of attorney shall not be effected by disability of the principal," or "this power of attorney should become effective upon the disability of the principal";

    b) the appointed decision maker may direct the utilization or withdrawal of medical procedures;

c) court-approved use of power of attorney to make health care decisions which involve termination of treatment.

11. There is case law supporting non-statutory directives.

CONNECTICUT

1. Provides a model Living Will/Treatment Directive.

2. Living Will prepared "may substantially" follow the model.

3. Person making the Living Will must be an adult, but there is no indication in the statute as to what age qualifies as such.

4. Person making a Living Will must be "of sound mind."

5. Living Will must be signed by two witnesses, but no other specifications are given regarding them.

6. Law provides a Living Will allows withdrawal of medical treatment when:

> a) diagnosis states declarant in a "terminal condition";
> b) diagnosis states declarant's condition is "incurable";
> c) diagnosis states declarant's condition is "irreversible."

7. Law says those medical procedures which can be removed are "life support systems" which are defined as any mechanical or electronic device, *excluding nutrition and hydration*, used to replace the function of vital organs, and which prolong the dying process.

8. Living Will is not to be in effect during a declarant's pregnancy.

9. There is case law supporting non-statutory directives.

DELAWARE

1. Provides "Death With Dignity Act," but does not, however, have a model Living Will/Treatment Directive.

2. Person must be an adult to execute a Living Will, but there is no indication in the statute as to what age qualifies.

3. Person making a Living Will must be "competent."

4. Living Will must be signed by two witnesses, who:

> a) are adults;
> b) must not be related to the declarant by blood or marriage;
> c) are not eligible to inherit from declarant;
> d) are not financially responsible for declarant's medical expenses;
> e) do not have a claim against the declarant's estate;
> f) must not be an employee of a health facility where the declarant is located.

5. Law provides a Living Will only allows withdrawal of medical treatment when:

> a) diagnosis states declarant is in a "terminal condition";
> b) diagnosis states declarant's "death is probable, whether or not medical treatment is used."

6. Law says those treatments which can be withdrawn are those which would only artificially prolong the dying process; *medication, however, may not be withdrawn.*

7 Living Will is not to be in effect during a declarant's pregnancy.

8. Provides for a health care proxy under the Living Will to make health care decisions for a declarant, which can include the withdrawal of treatment that would extend their life.

9. There is case law supporting non-statutory directives.

DISTRICT OF COLUMBIA

1. Provides a model Living Will/Treatment Directive.

2. Living Will prepared gives no specifications to follow model.

3. Person must be at least eighteen years of age to execute a Living Will.

4. Living Will may be executed by another person at the express direction of the declarant, in the declarant's presence.

5. Person making the Living Will must be "of sound mind."

6. Living Will must be signed by two witnesses, who must:

> a) not be related to declarant by blood or marriage;
> b) not be eligible to inherit from declarant;
> c) not be financially responsible for declarant's medical expenses;
> d) not have a claim against declarant's estate;
> e) not be the declarant's attending physician, his or her employee;
> f) not be an employee of a health facility.

7. If the person making the Living Will is in an intermediate care or skilled care facility, a directive is valid only when one of the witnesses to the directive is a patient advocate or ombudsman.

8. Laws provides a Living Will only allows withdrawal of medical treatment when:

> a) diagnosis states declarant in a "terminal condition";
> b) diagnosis must state declarant's condition "incurable";
> c) diagnosis must state "any treatment would only postpone the moment of death."

9. Law says those medical procedures which can be withdrawn are "those which would only artificially prolong the dying process; *administration of medication may not be withdrawn.*"

10. Provides a "District of Columbia Health Care Decision Act," entitled a "Durable Power of Attorney."

11. Provides a model form, but specifies that alternative language to the model form is not precluded by the statute.

12. Law states that the DPAHC document must be signed by two witnesses who:

    a) at least one is not related to declarant by either blood or marriage;

    b) at least one is not eligible to inherit from the declarant's estate;

    c) is not the declarant's health care provider, or an employee of such provider.

13. Law specifies that a declarant's health care provider may not be appointed as a decision maker.

14. There is case law supporting non-statutory directives.

FLORIDA

1. Provides a model Living Will/Treatment Directive.

2. Living Will prepared is not required to follow the model.

3. States that more specific directions may be included.

4. Person must be an adult to execute a Living Will, but there is no indication in the statute as to what age qualifies.

5. Person making the Living Will must be "competent."

6. Living Will must be signed by two witnesses who:

    a) one is neither a spouse or blood relative.

7. Law provides a Living Will only allows withdrawal of medical treatment when:

    a) diagnosis states declarant is in a "terminal condition";

    b) diagnosis states "death must be imminent."

8. Law says those medical procedures which can be withdrawn are those which replace spontaneous bodily functions, and which would only artificially prolong the dying process. *Nutrition and hydration may also be withdrawn, and a next of kin has the right to negate the removal of artificial feeding.*

9. Living Will is not to be in effect during pregnancy.

10. Provides a "Durable Power of Attorney Act" that calls for a Family Durable Power of Attorney, by which a spouse, parent, child, brother, sister, niece or nephew may become an attorney in fact.

11. Model form is not provided, but specifies that:

    a) document should note relationship between the declarant and the person appointed as DPAHC;

    b) document needs to include the words "this durable family power of attorney shall not be affected by the disability of the principal, except as provided by statute."

12. There is case law supporting non-statutory directives.

GEORGIA

1. Provides a model Living Will/Treatment Directive.

2. Living Will prepared is not required to follow the model.

3. Person must be an adult to execute a Living Will, and is so defined as an individual at least eighteen years of age.

4. Statute requires the person making the Living Will must be "of sound mind."

5. Requires that the Living Will be signed by two witnesses, who are:

  a) competent adults;
  b) not related to the declarant by blood or marriage;
  c) not eligible to inherit from the person's estate;
  d) not financially responsible for the declarant's medical expenses;
  e) not claimants against the declarant's estate;
  f) not the declarant's attending physician, or declarant's employee;
  g) not an employee of a health facility where the declarant is located.

6. If person making Living Will is in hospital or skilled-care facility, the Living Will is valid only with an additional witness beyond the two normally required, who is either:

  a) a physician on the hospital medical staff, not participating in the declarant's care;
  b) or a physician on the hospital medical staff of the skilled-care facility.

7. Law provides a Living Will only allows withdrawal of medical treatment when:

  a) diagnosis states declarant is in a "terminal condition";
  b) diagnosis states declarant's condition is "incurable";
  c) diagnosis states "death must be imminent."

8. Law says those medical procedures which can be withdrawn are those which would only artificially prolong the dying process; *nourishment, may not be withdrawn.*

9. Living Will not to be in effect during declarant's pregnancy.

10. Law provides a Living Will shall be effective for a period of seven years from the date of execution.

11. Provides a "Durable Power of Attorney for Health Care Act."

12. Provides a model form.

13. Law specifies Act is not intended to be exclusive method of delegating decision making decisions, and does not say form has to be used.

14. Provides that the DPAHC document needs:

> a) two competent adult witnesses sign it;
> b) signature of the attending physician, if declarant is in hospital or skilled-nursing facility;
> c) not to have the appointed decision maker be a health-care provider directly or indirectly involved with the declarant's treatment.

15. There is case law supporting non-statutory directives.

HAWAII

1. Provides a model Living Will/Treatment Directive.

2. Living Will prepared may, but need not, follow the model.

3. Person who has reached the age of majority may execute a Living Will, but there is no indication of what age qualifies.

4. Person making the Living Will must be "competent."

5. Living Will must be signed by two witnesses, who must:

> a) be eighteen years of age or older;
> b) not be related to declarant by blood, marriage, or adoption;
> c) not be an attending physician, declarant's employee, or employee of a health-care facility where the declarant is located.

6. Law provides a Living Will only allows withdrawal of "life-sustaining procedures" when:

> a) diagnosis states declarant is in a "terminal condition";
> b) diagnosis must state declarant's condition "incurable";
> c) diagnosis must state "death likely to occur in a relatively short time."

7. Law says those medical procedures which can be withdrawn are those which would only artificially prolong the dying process.

8. Law does not specifically address pregnancy, but the model Living Will provides that it is not operative during period when declarant is pregnant.

9. Law provides a "Uniform Durable Power of Attorney Act."

10. Provides no model form, but does state that on document should appear:

> a) "this power of attorney shall not be effected by the disability of the principal," or
> b) "this power of attorney should become effective upon the disability of the principal."

11. There is case law supporting non-statutory directives.

IDAHO

1. Provides a model Living Will/Treatment Directive.

2. Living Will prepared "must be in same form" as the model or in a form which contains the same elements.

3. Provides any "competent person" may execute a Living Will, that is "either as an emancipated minor, or is at least eighteen years of age, and is of sound mind."

4. Living Will must be signed by two witnesses at least eighteen years of age, but no other specifications are given regarding them.

5. Law provides a Living Will only allows withdrawal of medical treatment when:

> a) diagnosis states "death is imminent";
>
> b) diagnosis states treatment would "only postpone dying process";
>
> c) diagnosis states declarant is "in a persistent vegetative state."

6. "Natural Death Act" also provides the appointment of an "attorney-in-fact/proxy" who can make health-care decisions regarding life-sustaining treatment when the declarant is not able to make such decisions.

7. There is no case law supporting non-statutory directives.

INDIANA

1. Provides a model Living Will/Treatment Directive.

2. Living Will prepared "must be in substantially the same form," although it may include more specific directions.

3. Provides "any person at least eighteen years old and of sound mind may execute a Living Will."

4. Living Will must be signed by two witnesses, who must:

    a) not have signed the Living Will on behalf of the declarant;

    b) not be a parent, spouse or child of the declarant;

    c) not be eligible to inherit from the declarant's estate;

    d) not be financially responsible for the declarant's medical expenses.

5. Law provides a Living Will only allows withdrawal of medical treatment when:

    a) diagnosis states declarant is in a "terminal condition";

    b) diagnosis states "there is no possibility of recovery";

    c) diagnosis states "death will occur within a short period of time without medical treatment."

6. Law says those medical procedures which can be withdrawn are "those which replace a vital bodily function, and which would only artificially prolong the dying process.

A Living Will prepared under this section does not require that a doctor withhold medical treatment, but merely represents strong evidence of the patient's intentions.

The law also provides a Living Will which requests that life-sustaining procedures be maintained even if a person is in a terminal condition."

7. Provides for a health-care proxy to be appointed by a declarant, to be consulted by a doctor as "to the intent and validity of the Living Will."

8. There is no case law supporting non-statutory directives.

ILLINOIS

1. Provides a model Living Will/Treatment Directive.

2. Living Will prepared "need not be" in same form specified in the model.

3. Person making Living Will must be "of sound mind, who has reached the age of majority, or who is an emancipated minor."

4. Living Will must be signed by two witnesses at least eighteen years of age, but there are no other specifications given regarding them.

5. Law provides a Living Will only allows withdrawal of medical treatment when:

> a) diagnosis states declarant is in a "terminal condition";
> b) diagnosis states declarant's condition "incurable";
> c) diagnosis states declarant's condition "irreversible";
> d) diagnosis states "death must be imminent."

6. Law says those medical procedures which can be withdrawn are "those which would only artificially prolong the dying process. *Nutrition and hydration may not be withdrawn if the cause of death would be starvation or dehydration.*

7. "Powers of Attorney Health Care Act" provides a model form, but states that the Act is "not intended to be the exclusive method of delegating decision-making powers.

8. DPAHC document should be signed by one competent adult witness, but no other specifications are given regarding them.

9. There is case law supporting non-statutory directives.

IOWA

1. Provides a model Living Will/Treatment Directive.

2. Living Will prepared "need not be" in the same form as model.

3. Person must be an adult to execute a Living Will, but there is no indication in the statute as to what age qualifies.

4. Person making the Living Will must be "competent."

5. Living Will must be signed by two witnesses, but no other specifications are given regarding them.

6. Law provides a Living Will only allows withdrawal of medical treatment when:

    a) diagnosis states declarant is in a "terminal condition";

    b) diagnosis states declarant's condition is "incurable";

    c) diagnosis states declarant's condition is "irreversible";

    d) diagnosis states declarant "will die in a short period of time."

7. Law says those medical procedures which can be withdrawn are "those which would replace a spontaneous bodily function, and would only artificially prolong the dying process."

8. Living Will is not to be in effect during a declarant's pregnancy.

9. Law says life-sustaining procedure can be withheld from a patient who is not able to make health-care decisions, by the following individuals, with the restriction that a person subsequent on the list can only make a decision if the persons preceding them are not reasonably available for consultation:

    a) individual with power of attorney, if one has been appointed;

    b) legal guardian;

    c) patient's spouse;

    d) patient's adult child or, if there is more than one, a majority of the patient's adult children who are reasonably available;

    e) parent of the patient, or both parents;

    f) patient's adult sibling

10. "Powers of Attorney Act" authorizes declarant

to appoint another person legal powers if he or she becomes incompetent.

11. Model form is not provided, but specifies that on document should appear:

    a) "this power of attorney shall not be effected by disability of the principal" or

    b) "this power of attorney should become effective upon the disability of the principal."

12. Act does not specify that the appointed decision maker may direct withdrawal of medical procedures; however, the Iowa Life-Sustaining Procedures Act allows decisions regarding life-sustaining procedures to be made by an appointed decision maker if there is no Living Will.

13. There is no case law supporting non-statutory directives.

KANSAS

1. Provides a model Living Will/Treatment Directive.

2. Living Will prepared "should be substantially" the same as the model.

3. States that more specific directions may be included.

4. Person must be an adult to execute a Living Will, but there is no indication in the statute as to what age qualifies.

5. Model provides declarant is "emotionally and mentally competent," and this must be confirmed by two witnesses, who must sign and:

    a) not have signed Living Will on behalf of declarant;

    b) are not related to declarant by either blood or marriage;

    c) are not eligible to inherit from declarant's estate;

    d) are not financially responsible for declarant's medical expenses.

6. Law provides a Living Will only allows withdrawal of medical treatment when:

    a) diagnosis states declarant is in a "terminal condition."

7. Law says those medical procedures which can be withdrawn are "those which would only prolong the dying process."

8. Provides a "Durable Power of Attorney for Health-Care Decisions Act."

9. Provides a model form, and does provide that:

    a) on it appear phrase, "this power of attorney for health-care decisions shall not be effected by subsequent disability or incapacity of the principal" or "this power of attorney for health care shall become effective upon the disability or incapacity of the principal";

    b) appointed decision maker may direct the withdrawal of medical procedures; however, the Iowa Life-Sustaining Procedures Act allows decisions regarding life-sustaining procedures to be made by an appointed decision maker if there is no Living Will;

   c) DPAHC document should be prepared with
    the same formality as a Living Will under
    the Kansas Natural-Death Act.

  10. There is no case law supporting non-statutory
directives.

KENTUCKY

1. Provides a model Living Will/Treatment Directive.

2. Living Will prepared "should be substantially" the same as the model.

3. States that more specific directions may be included.

4. Person must be an adult to execute a Living Will, but there is no indication in the statute as to what age qualifies.

5. Person making the Living Will must be "emotionally and mentally competent," and this must be confirmed by two witnesses, who must indicate this on the Living Will, and they must:

> a) not be related to the declarant by blood;
> b) not be employed by a health-care facility in which the declarant is residing;
> c) not be the declarant's attending physician;
> d) not be eligible to inherit from the declarant's estate;
> e) not be financially responsible for the declarant's medical expenses.

6. Law provides a Living Will only allows the withdrawal of medical treatment when:

> a) diagnosis states declarant is in a "terminal condition";
> b) diagnosis states declarant's "death is likely to occur in a relatively short time."

7. Law says those medical procedures which can be withdrawn are "those which would only prolong the dying process."

8. Provides a "Health-Care Surrogate Act."

9. Does provide at model form, but states "one substantially in the same form and having other specific instructions not inconsistent with the Act may be provided."

10. Provides that the DPAHC document must:

> a) be signed by two competent adult witnesses, or notarized by a notary public or other person authorized to administer oaths;
> b) not be signed by the operator or employee of a hospital or skilled-nursing facility in which declarant is located, unless the

> declarant and the witness are related;
>> c) not have any such health-care provider appointed the declarant's decision maker.

11. Provides that the DPAHC may not request the withdrawal of nutrition and hydration, except in specified circumstances.

12. Life-sustaining treatment and nutrition and hydration must be provided during a declarant's pregnancy.

13. There is no case law supporting non-statutory directives.

LOUISIANA

1. Provides a model Living Will/Treatment Directive.

2. Living Will prepared is not required to follow the model.

3. Person must be an adult to execute a Living Will, but there is no indication in the statute as to what age qualifies.

4. Person making the Living Will must be "emotionally and mentally competent," and this must be confirmed by two witnesses who must:

> a) be competent adults;
> b) not be related to the declarant by either blood or by marriage:
> c) not be eligible to inherit from declarant.

5. Law provides a Living Will can be prepared for an incompetent, terminally-ill patient, by the first person on the following list who is reasonably available for consultation:

> a) judicially appointed tutor or curator, if one has been appointed;
> b) patient's spouse;
> c) patient's adult child;
> d) parents of a patient:
> e) patient's siblings;
> f) patient's ascendant or descendants;
> g) and if more than one person is reasonably available in any of the above, then the decision shall be made by all of the persons of that class.

6. Law provides a Living Will can be prepared for a minor who is terminally ill by the first person on the following list who is reasonably available for consultation:

> a) a spouse who has reached "the state of majority";
> b) the parent or guardian of a patient.

It is to be noted that such a decision cannot be against the previously expressed desire of the minor, nor can such a decision be made by a parent or guardian against the express wishes of a spouse, parent or guardian.

7. Law provides a Living Will only allows withdrawal of medical treatment when: diagnosis states declarant is in a "terminal and irreversible" condition.

8. Law says those medical procedures which can

be withdrawn are "those which would only artificially prolong the dying process.

9. Law provides that a Living Will may also contain the appointment of a health-care proxy.

10. There is no case law supporting non-statutory directives.

MAINE

1. Provides a model Living Will/Treatment Directive.

2. Living Will prepared "may, but need not," be in the same form as model.

3. Any person "over eighteen" may execute a Living Will.

4. Person making the Living Will must be "of sound mind and emotionally and mentally competent."

5. Living Will must be signed by two witnesses, but no other specifications are given regarding them.

6. Law provides a Living Will allows withdrawal of medical treatment when:

> a) diagnosis states declarant is in a "terminal condition";
>
> b) diagnosis states declarant's death is likely to occur in a relatively short time.

7. Law says those medical procedures which can be withdrawn are "those which would only prolong the dying process." *In addition, a declarant can also elect for withdrawal of nutrition and hydration in the event of terminal illness.*

8. Law provides for appointment of a health-care proxy under a Living Will to make medical decisions for the declarant.

9. Provides a "Powers of Attorney Act," by which an individual may appoint another to exercise the declarant's legal powers if the declarant becomes incompetent.

10. Does not provide a model form, but does provide that:

> a) on it appear that "this power of attorney shall not be effected by disability of the principal; or
>
> b) on it appear that "this power of attorney should become effective upon the disability of the principal."

11. Law provides that the appointed decision maker may direct the utilization or withdrawal of medical procedures.

12.   There is case law supporting non-statutory directives

MARYLAND

1. Provides a model Living Will/Treatment Directive.

2. Living Will prepared "must be" in the form of the model provided.

3. States that "any individual who is qualified to make a will in Maryland may execute a Living Will."

4. Requires that the Living Will be signed by two witnesses who:

> a) are at least eighteen years old;
> b) did not sign the Living Will for the declarant;
> c) are not related to the person by either blood or marriage;
> d) are not eligible to inherit from the declarant's
> e) are not financially or otherwise responsible for the declarant's medical treatment;
> f) do not have a claim against the declarant's estate.

5. Law provides a Living Will only allows withdrawal of medical treatment when:

> a) diagnosis states declarant is in a "terminal condition";
> b) diagnosis states declarant's conditions is incurable;
> c) diagnosis states declarant's death is imminent.

6. Law says those medical procedures which can be withdrawn are "those which would supplant a vital bodily function, and would secure only a "precarious and burdensome" prolongation of life.

7. Living Will is not to be in effect during a declarant's pregnancy.

8. Provides a "Durable Power of Attorney Act."

9. Provides no model form, but does provide that:

> a) on it appear "this power of attorney shall not be effected by disability of the principal"; or
> b) on it appear "this power of attorney should become effective upon the disability of the principal."

11. New law requires that a decision to withdraw medical treatment for a disabled person requires a court order.

12. There is no case law supporting non-statutory directives.

MASSACHUSETTS

1. Statute provides no model form for a Living Will.

2. Provides for the appointment of a health-care agent by creation of a health-care proxy, "which may become effective upon a determination that the declarant lacks the capacity to make health-care decisions" whose powers:

   a) are deemed as broad as the powers of the declarant unless otherwise limited by the proxy declaration;

   b) to make their decisions in accordance with the wishes of the declarant or, if those wishes are unknown, in the best wishes of the declarant.

3. There is case law supporting non-statutory directives.

MICHIGAN

There is case law supporting non-statutory directives which would appear to support a patient's right to refuse treatment, and consequently, a patient's right to have a Directive enforced if he or she is incompetent.

The state has no Living Will law.

MINNESOTA

1.Provides a model Living Will/Treatment Directive.

2. States that more specific directions may be included.

3. Person must be an adult to execute a Living Will, but there is no indication in the statute as to what age qualifies.

4. Person making the Living Will must be "of sound mind."

5. Living Will must be signed by two witnesses, who must:

        a) not be entitled to inherit from declarant;
        b) not be designated as a medical proxy for the declarant.

6. Law does not limit implementation of refusal or withdrawal of medical care to persons in a "terminal condition."

7. Law provides for appointment of a health-care proxy, either to enforce specific instructions or to make medical decisions without instructions. However, it states that "absent explicit authorization," the health-care proxy may not consent to the withdrawal of nutrition and hydration.

8.   There is case law supporting non-statutory directives.

MISSISSIPPI

1. Provides a model Living Will/Treatment Directive.

2. Living Will prepared "must follow substantially" the model form provided.

3. Person must be at least eighteen years of age to execute a Living Will.

4. Persons making the Living Will must be "mentally competent."

5. Living Will must be signed by two witnesses who must be:

> a) not related to declarant by blood or marriage;
> b) not entitled to inherit from declarant;
> c) not have a claim against declarant's estate;
> d) not be the declarant's physician or an employee of such physician.

6. Law provides a Living Will only allows withdrawal of medical treatment "if death is imminent."

7. Living Will is not to be in effect during a declarant's pregnancy.

8. Provides a "Durable Power of Attorney for Health Care Act."

9. Provides a model form, and requires witness statements and notary public affirmations.

10. Act does require that the document specifically authorize the decision maker to determine health care decisions, and that they:

> a) cannot be a treating health-care provider;
> b) cannot be an employee of a treating health-care provider.

11. Provides that the DPAHC document needs two competent witnesses who are:

> a) not health-care providers;
> b) not employees of a health-care provider;
> c) not the appointed decision maker;
> d) not related to the declarant by blood or marriage;
> e) not entitled to inherit from the declarant.

12. There is no case law supporting non-statutory directives.

MISSOURI

1. Provides a model Living Will/Treatment Directive.

2. Living Will prepared "need not be" in the same form as the model.

3. Person making the Living Will must be at least eighteen years of age or older.

4. Person making the Living Will must be competent, "of sound mind," and able "to receive and evaluate information and communicate a decision."

5. Living Will must be signed by two witnesses who must:

> a) be eighteen years of age;
> b) not have signed the Living Will on the declarant's behalf.

6. Law provides a Living Will only allows withdrawal of "death-prolonging procedures" when:

> a) diagnosis states declarant is in a "terminal condition";
> b) diagnosis states declarant's condition is "incurable";
> c) diagnosis states declarant's condition is "irreversible";
> d) diagnosis states declarant's death "will occur in a short period of time."

7. There is case law supporting non-statutory directives. This is the now-famous *Cruzan v. Director, Missouri Department of Health.*

MONTANA

1. Provides a model Living Will/Treatment Directive.

2. Living Will prepared "need not be" in the form of the model.

3. Person must be an adult to execute a Living Will, but there is no indication in the statute as to what age qualifies.

4. Person making the Living Will must be "competent."

5. Living Will must be signed by two witnesses, but no other specifications are given regarding them.

6. Law provides a Living Will only allows "withdrawal of life-sustaining procedures" when:

      a) diagnosis states declarant is "terminally ill";

      b) diagnosis states declarant's condition is "incurable";

      c) diagnosis states declarant's condition is "irreversible";

      d) diagnosis states declarant's "death will occur in a relatively short period of time."

7. Living Will is not to be implemented if the person is pregnant.

8. There is no case law supporting non-statutory directives.

NEVADA

1. Provides a model Living Will/Treatment Directive.

2. Living Will prepared "must be substantially" the same as model form.

3. Person must be an adult to execute a Living Will, but there is no indication in the statute as to what age qualifies.

4. Person making the Living Will must be "of sound mind."

5. Living Will must be signed by two witnesses "in the same manner in which a will is executed," and who must be:

> a) not related to the declarant by blood or marriage;
>
> b) not have a claim against the estate of the declarant;
>
> c) not be an attending physician, the employee of an attending physician of the declarant;
>
> d) not be an employee of a health facility in which the declarant is a patient.

6. Law says those medical procedures which can be withdrawn are "life-sustaining procedures."

7. Living Will is to be void during a declarant's pregnancy.

8. "Durable Power of Attorney for Health Care Act" provides a model form.

9. Law states that under this statute an Appointment Directives must be substantially in the same form.

10. DPAHC document must be notarized by a notary public.

11. DPAHC document must be signed by two witnesses who must:

> a) not be related by blood or marriage to the declarant;
>
> b) not be entitled to inherit from the declarant;
>
> c) not be the declarant's decision maker;
>
> d) not be a health-care provider or their employers or operators where the declarant is a patient.

12. If the declarant is in a skilled-nursing facility, the Appointment Directive must be signed by a patient advocate or ombudsman.

13. Law forbids the appointment of a power of attorney to health-care providers who provide treatment to a declarant, the provider's employees, or any employees or operator of a health-care facility.

14. There is no case law supporting non-statutory directives.

NEW HAMPSHIRE

1. Provides a model Living Will/Treatment Directive.

2. Living Will "may, but need not," follow the model.

3. Person who is at least eighteen years old may execute a Living Will.

4. Person making the Living Will must be "of sound mind."

5. Requires that the Living Will must be signed by two witnesses who:

> a) are not related to the declarant;
> b) are not eligible to inherit from the declarant;
> c) do not have a claim against the declarant's estate;
> d) are not the declarant's physician or his or her employee.

6. Law states that the Living Will must be notarized.

7. Laws provides that if the declarant executing the Living Will is a patient in a hospital or skilled-nursing facility, then the Living Will must be signed in the presence of the chief of the hospital medical staff or the medical director of the nursing facility where the patient is located.

8. Law provides a Living Will allows a person may direct the withdrawal of "life-sustaining procedures" when:

> a) diagnosis states declarant is in a "terminal condition";
> b) diagnosis states declarant's condition is "incurable";
> c) diagnosis states declarant's death is "imminent."

9. Law says those life-sustaining procedures which can be withdrawn are "those which artificially prolong life." *Medication or sustenance may not be withdrawn.*

10. Living Will is not to be in effect during a declarant's pregnancy.

11. There is no case law supporting non-statutory directives.

NEW JERSEY

1. Provides for a Durable Power of Attorney appointment, but does not provide a model DPAHC document.

2. Law says the DPAHC:
   a) may exercise the declarant's legal power if he or she becomes incompetent.
   b) shall not be effected by disability of the principal;
   c) should become effective upon the disability of the principal.

3. Law does not specifically provide the authority for the appointed decision maker to make decisions regarding medical procedures.

4. There is case law supporting non-statutory directives.

NEW MEXICO

1. Statute provides no model form for a Living Will.

2. Provides that anyone who has reached the age of majority may execute a Living Will, but there is no indication in the statue as to at what age a person reaches majority.

3. Person making the Living Will must be "of sound mind."

4. Living Will must be "executed with the same formality as a will."

5. Living Will may be executed on behalf of a minor who has been certified as suffering from either:
   a) terminal illness; or
   b) in an irreversible coma.

6 The following persons may execute the Living Will on the minor's behalf:
   a) spouse, if he or she has reached "the age of majority";
   b) if no spouse, or the spouse is unavailable at the time of the certification, then either the parent or guardian of the minor.

7. Living Will may not be executed on a minor's behalf by "such" persons if:
   a) they are aware that the minor does not agree with the action;
   b) the execution is being done by a parent or guardian, and they are aware that either

another guardian or a spouse of the proposed declarant who has "attained the age of majority" objects to a Living Will being executed on the minor'sbehalf.

8. A Living Will executed on a minor's behalf must be done with the same formalities as a will, and must be certified by a district court judge.

9. A Living Will may be executed on behalf of an incompetent person who has been certified as:
   a) terminally ill, or
   b) in an irreversible coma.

10. A Living Will executed on behalf of an incompetent person certified as being of one of two conditions, requires agreement of "all family members reasonably available."

11. Law provides a Living Will only allows the withdrawal of "maintenance medical treatment" when:
   a) diagnosis states declarant in a "terminal condition";
   b) diagnosis states declarant in an "irreversible coma."

12. Law says those "maintenance medical treatments" which can be withdrawn are "those which are designed solely to sustain the life processes."

13. "The New Mexico Act" provides for a general power of attorney, by which an individual may appoint another to exercise the declarant's legal powers if the declarant becomes incompetent.

14. The statute does provide an optional model form by which to execute this Power of Attorney. While the form is optional, the statute specifies that:
   a) on it appear: "this power of attorney shall not be effected by disability of the principal"; or
   b) on it appear: "this power of attorney should become effective upon the disability of the principal."

15. The model Directive provides the authority for the appointed decision maker to determine decisions regarding medical procedures.

16. The statute states that the Appointment Directive should be notarized.

17. There is no case law supporting non-statutory directives.

NEW YORK

1. Provides for a health-care proxy to be appointed, but does not provide a model Living Will/Treatment Directive.

2. Law requires the proxy:
   a) shall be signed by two witnesses;
   b) may not be operator, administrator or employee of a hospital where the declarant is located, unless they are related to the declarant;
   c) may not be a physician affiliated with a facility where the declarant is located;
   d) who is a non-relative, may not be appointed as health-care agent for more than ten declarants;
   e) if executed in a mental hygiene facility, have additional qualified witnesses.

3. Law does not limit authority of the agent, except that the agent must have a basis for knowing that a patient would not want artificial nutrition and hydration, and instructions so regarding should be on the form.

4. There is case law supporting non-statutory directives.

NORTH CAROLINA

1. Provides a model Living Will/Treatment Directive "that is specifically determined to fulfill the requirements of the statute."

2. The statute does not specifically require a minimum age or level of maturity necessary for a person to execute a directive.

3. Person making the Living Will must be "of sound mind," and this must be confirmed by two witnesses who sign and must:

> a) not be related to the declarant by blood or marriage;
>
> b) not be eligible to inherit from declarant;
>
> c) do not have a claim against the estate of the declarant;
>
> d) not be the declarant's attending physician, and neither be his or her employee;
>
> e) not be an employee of a health-care facility where the declarant is a patient.

4. Statute requires the Living Will must be approved by:

> a) a clerk,
>
> b) an assistant clerk of a superior court, or
>
> c) a notary public.

5. Statue provides that a declarant can direct that "extraordinary means" not be used if the person is in a terminal condition and is incurable.

"Extraordinary means" is defined as a medical procedure which would replace a vital function, and would only artificially postpone the moment of death.

6. The North Carolina Power of Attorney Act provides a general power of attorney, by which an individual may appoint another to exercise the declarant's legal powers if the declarant becomes incompetent.

7. The North Carolina Power of Attorney states that on document "should appear" the phrase:

> a) "this power of attorney shall not be effected by subsequent incapacity or mental incompetency"; or
>
> b) "this power of attorney shall become effective after I become incapacitated or mentally incompetent."

8. The Act does not specifically address whether the appointed decision makers may direct the utilization or withdrawal of medical procedures.

9. There is no case law supporting non-statutory directives.

NORTH DAKOTA

1. Provides a model Living Will/Treatment Directive.

2. Living Will prepared "must be" substantially the same.

3. States that more specific instructions may be added.

4. Person who is at least eighteen may execute a "Living Will."

5. Person making the Living Will must be "of sound mind."

6. Living Will must be signed by two witnesses who must:

> a) not be related to declarant by blood or marriage;
>
> b) not be eligible to inherit from declarant's estate;
>
> c) not be financially responsible for declarant's medical expenses;
>
> d) not have a claim against the declarant's estate;
>
> e) not be the declarant's attending physician.

7. If the declarant is in a long-term-care facility at the time the Living Will is executed, one of the two witnesses must be a regional long-term-care ombudsman.

8. Statute provides that a declarant can direct the withdrawal of "life-prolonging treatment" when:

> a) diagnosis states declarant is in a "terminal condition";
>
> b) diagnosis states declarant's death is imminent;
>
> c) diagnosis states declarant' condition is incurable.

The statute specifically provides that terminal conditions will not include specified chronic or comatose conditions.

9. Living Will is not to be in effect during a declarant's pregnancy, unless "such treatment will not permit the continued development and live birth of a child, or the treatment will be physically harmful or unreasonably painful, or it will prolong severe pain which cannot be treated by medication.

10. There is case law supporting non-statutory directives.

OHIO

1. Provides for an Appointment Directive for health-care decisions based on a general durable power of attorney, but provides no model form, and does not provide a statute or form on Living Wills.

2. Provides that an Appointment Directive must "be either notarized by a notary public or must be signed by two witnesses who are:

> a) not related to the declarant by blood or marriage;
>
> b) not eligible "to benefit" from declarant's death;
>
> c) not the appointed decision maker for the declarant;
>
> d) not the declarant's physician or agent;
>
> e) not a health-care provider or their agent.

3. Specifies that an Appointment Directive expires after seven years.

4. Qualifies that the appointed decision maker may not be:

> a) an attending physician, or his or her agent, caring for the declarant;
>
> b) an employee of a health-care facility where the declarant is located.

5. Determines that the appointed decision maker is:

> a) not to request the withdrawal of medical treatment which will result in death, "unless the declarant is terminally ill";
>
> b) to "be restricted in power" to withdraw medical treatment which will result in death if the declarant is pregnant;
>
> c) *restricted as to their ability to refuse nutrition and hydration.*

6. There is case law supporting non-statutory directives.

OKLAHOMA

1. Provides a model Living Will/Treatment Directive.

2. Living Will prepared "must be substantially" the same form as the model.

3. States that more specific instructions may be added.

4. Person who is at least twenty-one years of age may execute a Living Will.

5. Person making a Living Will must be "of sound mind."

6. Living Will must be signed by two witnesses who must be:

> a) twenty-one years of age or older;
> b) not related to the declarant by blood or marriage;
> c) not be eligible to inherit from declarant's estate;
> d) not be financially responsible for declarant's medical expenses;
> e) not have a claim against the declarant's estate;
> f) not be the declarant's attending physician, nor his or her employee;
> g) not be an employee of a health-care facility where the declarant is located;
> h) not be another patient in a health-care facility where the declarant is located.

7. Law provides a Living Will allows withdrawal of "life-prolonging treatment" when:

> a) diagnosis states declarant is in a "terminal condition";
> b) diagnosis states declarant's death is to occur in hours or days (and this must be certified);
> c) diagnosis states declarant's condition is "incurable."

8. Law provides that declarant must specify if he or she wants *nutrition* and *hydration* to be withdrawn, if terminally ill.

9. There is no case law supporting non-statutory directives.

OREGON

1. Provides a model Living Will/Treatment Directive.

2. Living Will prepared "must be the same" as the model.

3. Person must be at least eighteen years old to execute a Living Will.

4. Person making the Living Will must be "of sound mind."

5. Living Will must be signed by two witnesses who must:

> a) not be related to declarant by blood or marriage;
> b) not be eligible to inherit from declarant's estate;
> c) not have a claim against the declarant's estate;
> d) not be the declarant's attending physician, nor his or her employee;
> e) not be an employee of the health-care facility where the declarant is located.

6. Statute qualifies that if an individual is in a long-term-care facility at the time the Living Will is executed, that one of the two witnesses to the Treatment Directive must be a person designated by the Oregon Department of Human Resources.

7. Law allows the withdrawal of "life-sustaining treatment" when:

> a) diagnosis states declarant is in a "terminal condition";
> b) diagnosis states declarant's condition "incurable."

8. Law states those medical procedures which can be withdrawn are "those which replace a vital function, and would only artificially prolong the dying process."

9. Statute permits life-sustaining procedures to be withdrawn if the patient is in a terminal condition and is permanently unconscious and no Living Will has been prepared, at the request of the first of the following, in the prescribed order, who can be located with reasonable effort:

> a) the patient's spouse;
> b) a guardian of the patient;

> c) a majority of adult children of the patient who can be located;
>
> d) either parent of the patient.

And if none of the above are available, then such decision can be made under the supervision of the attending physician.

10. The "Oregon Durable Power of Attorney for Health Care Act" provides a model form which must be used and must be prepared the same as the model Living Will.

11. The decision maker appointed in the Durable Power of Attorney for Health-Care Document/Appointment Directive being:

> a) not either the declarant's attending physician, or an employee of that physician;
>
> b) not an operator or employee of a health-care facility in which the declarant is located, unless that decision maker is a relative;
>
> c) not responsible for the declarant's health-costs.

12. The statute provides that the durable power of attorney shall be effective for seven years, unless re-executed.

13. Act provides that a decision maker may only request the withdrawal of life-sustaining procedure if:

> a) specifically authorized under the power of attorney;
>
> b) the declarant is irreversibly comatose, terminally ill, and the decision is approved by a hospital committee.

Nutrition and hydration may only be withdrawn if this is also specifically authorized by the power of attorney.

14. There is no case law supporting non-statutory directives.

PENNSYLVANIA

1. Provides for a general power of attorney under The Pennsylvania Durable Power of Attorney Act, but does not provide a model DPAHC document.

2. Law says the declarant may appoint another to exercise his or her legal power if incompetent, and that on the document should appear:

> a) "this power of attorney shall become effective after I become incapacitated or mentally incompetent"; or
>
> b) "this power of attorney shall not be effected by my subsequent disability or incapacity."

3. The Act does not specifically address whether the appointed decision makers may direct the utilization or withdrawal of medical procedures.

4. There is case law supporting non-statutory directives.

RHODE ISLAND

1. Provides for an Appointed Durable Power of Attorney for Health Care decision maker and document/Appointment Directive in a model form; *and is the only form which may be used, and may not be altered.*

2. Person making the Appointment Directive must be at least eighteen years old, *and a resident of Rhode Island.*

3. The Directive can contain specific instructions for care, which should then be carried out by the appointed decision maker.

4. The appointed decision maker may not be:
   a) a treating health-care provider;
   b) a non-relative employee of a treating health-care provider;
   c) an operator of a community-care facility;
   d) a non-relative employee of a community-care facility.

5. The Appointment Directive must be signed by two witnesses:
   a) at least one of whom must not be related to the declarant by blood, marriage or adoption, and such witness may not be entitled to inherit from declarant;
   b) neither of whom may be the designated decision maker;
   c) neither of whom may be an employee of a health-care provider;
   d) neither of whom may be an operator of a community care facility;
   e) neither of whom may be an employee of a community care facility;
   f) at least one of whom of the witnesses must be personally know to the declarant.

6. There is case law supporting non-statutory directives.

SOUTH CAROLINA

1. Provides a model Living Will/Treatment Directive.

2. Living Will prepared "must be substantially the same" as the model form.

3. Person must be at least eighteen years old to execute a Living Will.

4. Person making the Living Will must be "emotionally and mentally competent," and this must be confirmed by two witnesses, who must sign and:

> a) are not related to the declarant by blood or marriage;
>
> b) are not eligible to inherit from the declarant's estate;
>
> c) are not financially responsible for the declarant's medical treatment;
>
> d) are not a beneficiary of a life insurance policy on the declarant;
>
> e) do not have a claim against the declarant's estate;
>
> f) are not the declarant's attending physician, or that physician's employees.

However, an employee of the health-care facility where the declarant is located may be a witness, but only if the other witness is not an employee of the same health care facility.

5. If the person executing the Living Will is a patient in a hospital or skilled-nursing facility, the document must be witnessed and signed by an ombudsman designated by the Office of the Governor of South Carolina.

6. Law provides a Living Will only allows withdrawal of medical treatment when:

> a) diagnosis states declarant is in a "terminal condition";
>
> b) diagnosis states declarant's condition is "incurable";
>
> c) diagnosis states declarant's condition is "irreversible";
>
> d) diagnosis states declarant's death will occur in a relatively short time.

7. Law says those medical procedures which can be withdrawn are "those which would only prolong the dying process."

8. Law provides that a Living Will is not to be in effect during a declarant's pregnancy.

9. The South Carolina Power of Attorney Act

provides for a durable power of attorney, by which an individual may appoint another to exercise the declarant's legal powers if the declarant becomes incompetent, and requires the directive "should be executed with the same formalities as a will.

10. The statute:

    a) Provides that the phrase "this power of attorney shall not be affected by physical disability or mental incompetence of the principal which renders the principal incapable of managing his or her own estate," or similar language, should appear.

    b) Does not specifically provide the authority for the appointed decision maker to make decisions regarding medical procedures for the declarant.

11. There is no case law supporting non-statutory directives.

SOUTH DAKOTA

1. Provides for a power of attorney under the South Dakota Durable Powers of Attorney Act, but does not provide a model document.

2. Law says an individual may appoint another to exercise the declarant's legal powers if the declarant became incompetent, and that on the document should appear:

> a) "this power of attorney shall not be effected by disability of the principal"; or
>
> b) "this power of attorney shall become effective upon the disability of the principal."

3. The Act specifically provides that the appointed decision maker may make health-care decisions for the declarant, but is restricted in their ability to provide for the withdrawal of nutrition and hydration unless the power of attorney expressly grants that power or directs that result.

4. There is no case law supporting non-statutory directives.

TENNESSEE

1. Provides a model Living Will/Treatment Directive.

2. Living Will prepared "must be in substantially" the same as model form.

3. States that more specific directions may be included.

4. Person must be an adult to execute a Living Will, but there is no indication in the statute as to what age qualifies.

5. Person making the Living Will must be a "competent person," and is so defined as an individual who is able to understand and appreciate the nature and consequences of a decision to refuse or accept medical treatment.

6. Living Will must be signed by two witnesses who:
   a) must not be related to declarant by blood or marriage;
   b) are not eligible to inherit from the declarant's estate;
   c) do not have claim against the declarant's estate;
   d) are not the declarant's attending physician, or that physician's employees;
   e) are not employed by a health-care facility where the declarant is located.

7. The model Living Will appears to indicate that the document should be notarized by a notary public, although no specific language requires such.

8. Law provides a Living Will only allows withdrawal of medical treatment when "diagnosis states declarant is in a terminal condition; and "terminal condition" is defined as a condition which would cause death within a short period of time, whether or not medical treatment is provided.

9. *Law says that those medical procedures which can be withdrawn would include simple nourishment and fluids.*

10. Provides for a declarant to designate an appointed decision maker under the Tennessee Durable Power of Attorney for Health Care Act, but does not provide a model Directive.

11. The Act does include the form that a notary seal on the Directive should be in, or it must be signed by two witnesses who:

a) are not the appointed power of attorney;

b) are not a health-care provider or an employee of a health-care provider where the declarant is located;

c) are not an employee of a health-care institution where the declarant is located;

d) at least one of the witnesses must be unrelated to the declarant by blood, marriage or adoption, and may not be entitled to any part of the estate of the principal.

12. There is no case law supporting non-statutory directives.

TEXAS

1. Provides a model Living Will/Treatment Directive.

2. Living Will prepared "need not be" in the same form as model.

3. Law provides that "any competent adult person" may execute a Living Will," but there is no indication as to what age qualifies.

4. Law specifies that a Living Will may be executed on behalf of a minor who has a terminal condition by:

> a) the patient's spouse, if the spouse is an adult;
> b) the patient's parents;
> c) the patient's legal guardian.

5. Law specifies that a decision to withdraw life-sustaining procedures may be made by the attending physician and the patient's legal guardian based on knowledge of the patient's desires, if known, should a patient be incompetent, terminally ill, and not have executed a Living Will. The law further defines that this decision will be made, if there is no legal guardian, by the attending physician and at least two persons of the following categories, in the following priority:

> a) the patient's spouse;
> b) a majority of the patient's reasonably available adult children;
> c) the patient's parents; or
> d) the patient's nearest living relative.

6. Requires that the Living Will be signed by two witnesses who:

> a) are not related to the declarant by blood or marriage;
> b) are not eligible to inherit from the declarant's estate;
> c) do not have a claim against the declarant's estate;
> d) are not the declarant's attending physician, or the physician's employees;
> e) are not an employee of a health-care facility where the declarant is located;
> f) are not directly involved in the financial affairs of the facility where the declarant is located;
> g) are not patients of a facility where the declarant is located.

7. Law provides a Living Will only allows the with-drawal of medical treatment when:

> a) diagnosis states declarant is in a "terminal condition";
>
> b) diagnosis states declarant's "death must be produced regardless of the use of medical treatment."

8. Law says those "life-sustaining treatments" which would be allowed withdrawn are "those which would only artificially prolong the dying process of a declarant whose death is imminent."

9. Under the Act, life-prolonging treatment cannot be withdrawn from a pregnant woman.

10. The law provides that an individual creating a Living Will may appoint another individual to make health-care decisions in the even that the declarant becomes incompetent.

11. The Texas Durable Power of Attorney for Health Care Act specifically provides for an Appointment Directive, titled "Durable Power of Attorney for Health Care," and provides a model form.

12. Under this statute, an Appointment Directive "must be substantially" in the same form as the model.

13. The Appointment Directive must be notarized by a notary public, and signed by two witnesses who:

> a) may not be the declarant's appointed decisionmaker;
>
> b) may not be the declarant's health or residential care provider, or their employees;
>
> c) may not be the declarant's spouse;
>
> d) may not be eligible to inherit from declarant's estate.

14. The Act forbids the appointment of power of attorney to health-care providers who give treatment to a declarant, the provider's employees, or any employees or operator of a residential-care facility, unless the person is a relative.

15. There is no case law supporting non-statutory directives.

UTAH

1. Provides a model Living Will/Treatment Directive.

2. Living Will prepared "must be substantially the same" as the model form.

3. Person who is at least eighteen may execute a Living Will.

4. Person making the Living Will must be "of sound mind," and this must be confirmed by two witnesses who sign and:

      a) may not have signed Living Will on behalf of declarant;

      b) may not be related to declarant by blood or marriage;

      c) may not be financially responsible for declarant's medical expenses;d) may not be eligible to inherit from declarant's estate;

      e) may not have a claim against the declarant's estate;

      f) may not be an employee or other agent of a health-care facility that is caring for the declarant.

5. Law specifies that if a patient is incompetent, terminally ill, and has not executed a Living Will, a decision to withdraw life-sustaining procedures may be made by the agreement of:

      a) the attending physician;

      b) another physician;

      c) any of the following persons, in the following order, who is available, willing and competent to act:

            1) a legal guardian, or the person's spouse;

            2) a parent;

            3) the person's children eighteen years of age or older.

6. Law provides a Living Will only allows withdrawal of medical treatment when diagnosis states declarant is in a "terminal condition."

7. Law says those medical procedures which can be withdrawn are "those which would only artificially prolong the dying process."

8. Law also provides for a less restrictive Living Will, by which specific medical treatments can be either ac-

cepted or rejected.

9. Provides a model form for an Appointment Directive.

10. There is no case law supporting non-statutory directives.

VERMONT

1. Provides a model Living Will/Treatment Directive.

2. Living Will prepared "need not be" in the same form as the model.

3. Person who is at least eighteen years of age may execute a Living Will.

4. Person making the Living Will must be "of sound mind."

5. Living Will must be signed by two witnesses who must:

> a) not be the declarant's spouse;
>
> b) not be an heir to the declarant's estate;
>
> c) not have a claim against the declarant's estate;
>
> d) not be the declarant's physician, or anyone working under his or her direction.

6. Law provides a Living Will only allows withdrawal of medical treatment when:

> a) diagnosis states declarant is in a "terminal condition";
>
> b) diagnosis states declarant's condition is "incurable."

7. Law directs the withdrawal of those medical procedures of "extraordinary measures," and so defines them as "those which would replace a vital function, and which only postpone the moment of death."

8. The Vermont Durable Power of Attorney for Health Care Act specifically provides a model form for an Appointment Directive.

9. The Appointment Directive must be in substantially the same form as the model.

10. Person making an Appointment Directive must sign and acknowledge a disclosure statement.

11. Appointment Directive must be signed by two witnesses who must:

> a) not be the declarant's health- or residential-care provider, nor their employees;
>
> b) not be the declarant's appointed decision maker;
>
> c) not be the declarant's spouse;
>
> d) not be an heir of the declarant;

    e) not be eligible to inherit from the declarant;

    f) not have any claim against the declarant's estate.

12. Declarant in a skilled-nursing facility and executing an Appointment Directive must have it signed by:

    a) an ombudsman;

    b) a member of the clergy;

    c) an attorney;

    d) or other person appointed by a probate court, who explains the nature and effect of the durable power of attorney.

13. Law forbids the appointment of power of attorney for the declarant to:

    a) his or her health-care provider or the provider's employees (unless a relative of the declarant);

    b) any employees or operator of a residential-care provider or their employees where the declarant is located (unless a relative of the declarant).

14. There is no case law supporting non-statutory directives.

VIRGINIA

1. Provides a model Living Will/Treatment Directive.

2. Living Will prepared "need not be" in the same form as the model.

3. Person must be an adult to execute a Living Will, but there is no indication in the statute as to what age qualifies.

4. Person making the Living Will must be "competent."

5. Law provides that if a patient is over eighteen, unable to communicate, terminally ill and has not executed a Living will, a decision to withdraw life-sustaining procedures may be made by the agreement of the attending physician and any of the following persons, in the following order or priority, if no individual of the prior class is available, willing and competent to act:

> a) a legal guardian or committee of the patient, if one has been appointed;
>
> b) person designated by the patient, in writing;
>
> c) the patient's spouse;
>
> d) the patient's adult children, or by a majority of the children if there are more than one;
>
> e) the parents of the patient; or
>
> f) the nearest living relative of the patient.

No decision made by persons in categories c), d), e) and f) shall be effected unless at least two of the persons consent to withdraw, provided they are reasonably available.

6. Law provides a Living Will only allows withdrawal of medical treatment when:

> a) diagnosis states declarant is in a "terminal condition";
>
> b) diagnosis states declarant's condition is such that no recovery can be possible;
>
> c) diagnosis states declarant's death is imminent.

7. Law says those medical procedures which can be withdrawn are "those which replace a vital function, and which serve only to postpone the moment of death."

8. The law provides for a Living Will under which an individual may appoint a health-care proxy. This health-care proxy may direct the withdrawal of a "life-prolonging

procedure" under the above-noted restrictions; i.e., "life-prolonging procedures" may be withdrawn from an individual in "terminal condition."

9. "The Virginia Durable Power of Attorney Act" provides for a durable power of attorney, by which an individual may appoint another to exercise the declarant's legal powers if the declarant becomes incompetent. It does not provide a model form.

10. Law provides that the phrase "this power of attorney (or his authority) shall not terminate on disability of the principal," or similar language should, appear.

11. Law provides that the appointed decision maker may not be the attending physician or his employer.

12. Law provides that a physician may withhold medical treatment from an individual if they are authorized by an appointed decision maker specifically authorized to make such decisions under a durable power of attorney.

13. There is no case law supporting non-statutory directives.

WASHINGTON

1. Provides a model Living Will/Treatment Directive.

2. Living Will prepared "should be essentially" the same as model form.

3. States that more specific directions may be added.

4. Person must be an adult at least eighteen years of age to execute a Living Will.

5. Person making the Living Will must be "of sound mind," and this must be confirmed by two witnesses who sign and:

> a) may not be related by blood or marriage to the declarant;
> b) may not be eligible to inherit from declarant's estate;
> c) may not have a claim against the declarant's estate;
> d) may not be the declarant's attending physician, or his or her employees;
> e) may not be an employee of a health-care facility in which the declarant is located.

6. Law provides a Living Will only allows withdrawal of "life-sustaining procedures" when:

> a) diagnosis states declarant is in a "terminal condition";
> b) diagnosis states declarant's condition is "incurable."

7. Law says the withdrawal of "life-sustaining procedures" that are permitted are "those which replace a vital function and serve only to postpone the moment of death."

8. Living Will is not to be in effect during pregnancy.

9. The Washington Durable Power of Attorney/Health-Care Decision Act provides for an individual to designate an appointed decision maker, but does not provide a model form.

10. The statute:

> a) provides that the phrase "this power of attorney shall not be affected by disability of the principal," or "this power of attorney shall become effective upon the disability of the principal," or similar language, should appear;
> b) provides that a declarant may grant the authority for the appointed decision maker to make decisions regarding medical pro-

cedures;

    c) forbids the following from being the declarant's appointed decision maker:

        1) their physician;

        2) their physician's employees;

        3) the owner, administrator or employees of any health-care facility where the declarant is located, unless they are the spouse, brother, sister, or adult child of the declarant.

    11. There is case law supporting non-statutory directives.

WEST VIRGINIA

1. Provides a model Living Will/Treatment Directive.

2. Living Will prepared "should be in substantially" the same as model form.

3. States that more specific directions may be added.

4. Person must be an adult at least eighteen years of age to execute a Living Will.

5. Person making the Living Will must be "of sound mind," and this must be confirmed by the two witnesses who sign and:

> a) may not have signed the Living Will on the declarant's behalf;
>
> b) may not be related by blood or marriage to the declarant;
>
> c) may not be eligible to inherit from the declarant's estate (or are not aware that they have been made a beneficiary of the person's will;
>
> d) may not be directly financially responsible for the declarant;
>
> e) may not be the declarant's attending physician, or employees of that physician;
>
> f) may not be employed by a health-care facility in which the declarant is located.

6. The West Virginia Medical Power of Attorney for Health Care Act specifically provides for an Appointment Directive titled "Medical Power of Attorney," and does provide a model form.

7. The Appointment Directive under this statute must be substantially in the same form.

8. The Appointment Directive must be signed by two witnesses who:

> a) may not be related to declarant by blood or marriage;
>
> b) may not be entitled to inherit from declarant;
>
> c) may not be responsible for the declarant's medical expenses;
>
> d) may not be the declarant's physician;
>
> e) may not be the declarant's appointed decisionmaker;
>
> f) may not be employees or operators of a health-care facility where the declarant is located.

9. There is no case law supporting non-statutory directives.

WISCONSIN

1. Provides a model Living Will/Treatment Directive.

2. Although the Wisconsin Department of Health and Human Services is required to distribute copies of the model Living Will, it is not clear whether a Living Will may vary from the form.

3. Person must be at least eighteen years of age to execute a Living Will.

4. Person making the Living Will must be "of sound mind."

5. Living Will must be signed by two witnesses who must:

> a) not be related to declarant by blood or marriage;
> b) not be eligible to inherit form declarant's estate;
> c) not have a claim against declarant's estate;
> d) not be the declarant's attending physician or any employees of that physician;
> e) not be employees or nursing or medical staff of a health-care facility in which the declarant is located.

6. Law provides a Living Will only allows withdrawal of medical treatment when:

> a) diagnosis states declarant is in a "terminal condition";
> b) diagnosis states declarant's "death is imminent."

7. Law says those medical procedures which can be withdrawn are "those which serve only to prolong the dying process; *nutrition* and *hydration*, however, may not be withdrawn."

8. The Wisconsin Power of Attorney for Health Care Act provides a model form.

9. Law states that "distributions of the Appointment Directives set forth under this Act must be the same as the model."

10. Person executing an Appointment Directive must be at least eighteen years of age.

11. Person executing an Appointment Directive must be "of sound mind," and this must be confirmed by two witnesses who sign and:

> a) may not be related to the declarant by either blood or marriage or adoption;

> b) may not have knowledge that they are eligible to inherit from the declarant's estate;
> c) may not be financially responsible for the declarant's medical treatment;
> d) may not be an attending health-care provider for the declarant;
> e) may not be the declarant's appointed decisionmaker.

12. Law allows for the decision maker authority in withholding or withdrawal of medical treatment; *"with the exception that they must be explicitly authorized to require the withholding of non-oral nutrition and hydration; and* "in *addition, a decision maker is not effective during a declarant's pregnancy, unless this is specifically provided for under the Directive."*

13. There is no case law supporting non-statutory directives.

WYOMING

1. Provides a model Living Will/Treatment Directive.
2. Living Will prepared "need not be substantially" the same form as the model.
3. Person must be an adult to execute a Living Will, but there is no indication in the statute as to what age qualifies.
4. Living Will must be signed by two witnesses who must:
   a) not have signed the Living Will on behalf of the declarant;
   b) not be related to declarant by blood or marriage;
   c) not be eligible to inherit from declarant's estate;
   d) not be directly financially responsible for the declarant's health care.
5. Law provides for the withdrawal of "life-sustaining procedure" when:
   a) diagnosis states declarant is in a "terminal condition";
   b) diagnosis states declarant's condition is such that there is a reasonable certainty that recovery will not occur.
6. Law states that the withdrawal of "life-sustaining procedure" means those medical procedures which serve only to prolong the dying process.
7. There is no case law supporting non-statutory directives.

Following the state requirements to execute your Living Will and DPAHC documents should assure you that your collective advance directives will be followed. All of the actual model forms for states legislated have not been included because of frequent changes that might predate their intended value. They are easily obtainable through your attorney and the legal affairs office of your state capital.

However, I believe the following examples of Treatment Directives/Living Wills from the states of Florida, Virginia, and Hawaii provide an overview of legislated statutes.

FLORIDA - TREATMENT DIRECTIVE

Declaration

Declaration made this ____ day of _____, 19 __.

I, _____, willfully and voluntarily make known my desire that my dying not be artificially prolonged under the circumstances set forth below, and I do hereby declare:

If at any time I should have a terminal condition and if my attending physician has determined that there can be no recovery from such condition and that my death is imminent, I direct that life-prolonging procedures be withheld or withdrawn when the application of such procedures would serve only to prolong artificially the process of dying, and that I be permitted to die naturally with only the administration of medication or the performance of any medical procedure deemed necessary to provide me with comfort care or to alleviate pain.

In the absence of my ability to give directions regarding the use of such life-prolonging procedures, it is my intention that this declaration be honored by my family and physician as the final expression of my legal right to refuse medical or surgical treatment and to accept the consequences for such refusal.

If I have been diagnosed as pregnant and that diagnosis is known to my physician, this declaration shall have no force or effect during the course of my pregnancy.

I understand the full import of this declaration, and I am emotionally and mentally competent to make this declaration.

(Signed)_____

The declarant is known to me, and I believe him or her to be of sound mind.

_____

Witness

_____

Witness

HAWAII - TREATMENT DIRECTIVE

DECLARATION

A. Statement of Declarant

Declaration made this ___ day of ___ (month, year). I, _____, being of sound mind, wilfully and voluntarily make known my desire that my dying shall not be artificially prolonged under the circumstances set forth below, and do hereby declare:

If at any time I should have an incurable or irreversible condition certified to be terminal by two physicians who have personally examined me, one of whom shall be my attending physician, and the physicians have determined that I am unable to make decisions concerning my medical treatment, and that without administration of life-sustaining treatment my death will occur in a relatively short time, and where the application of life-sustaining procedures would serve only to prolong artificially the dying process, I direct that such procedures be withheld or withdrawn, and that I be permitted to die naturally with only the administration of medication, nourishment, or fluids or the performance of any medical procedure deemed necessary to provide me with comfort or to alleviate pain.

In the absence of my ability to give directions regarding the use of such life-sustaining procedures, it is my intention that this declaration shall be honored by my family and physician(s) as the final expressions of my legal right to refuse medical or surgical treatment and accept the consequences from such refusal.

I understand the full import of this declaration and I am emotionally and mentally competent to make this declaration.

Signed _____

Address _____

B. Statement of Witnesses

I am at least 18 years of age and

　　　　-not related to the declarant by blood,
　　　　marriage, or adoption; and
　　　　-not the attending physician, an employee of
　　　　the attending physician, or an employee of the
　　　　medical care facility in which the declarant
　　　　is a patient.

The declarant is personally known to me and I believe the declarant to be of sound mind.

Witness _____

Address _____

Witness _____

　　Address _____

C. Notarization

　　　　Subscribed and sworn to and acknowledged before me by _____, the declarant, and subscribed and sworn to before me by _____ and _____, witnesses, this ___ day of _____, 19 __.

　　(SEAL)　　Signed _____

　　　　　　　　_____

　　　　　　　　(Official capacity of officer)

[L 1986, c 338, pt of § 1]

VIRGINIA - TREATMENT DIRECTIVE

Declaration made this ___ day of ____ (month, year). I, _____, willfully and voluntarily make known my desire and do hereby declare:

CHOOSE ONLY ONE OF THE NEXT TWO PARAGRAPHS AND CROSS THROUGH THE OTHER

If at any time I should have a terminal condition and my attending physician has determined that there can be no recovery from such condition, my death is imminent, and I am comatose, incompetent or otherwise mentally or physically incapable of communication, I designate _____ to make a decision on my behalf as to whether life prolonging procedures shall be withheld or withdrawn. In the even that my designee decides that such procedures should be withheld or withdrawn, I wish to be permitted to die naturally with only the administration of medication or the performance of any medical procedure deemed necessary to provide me with comfort care or to alleviate pain.

OR

If at any time I should have a terminal condition and my attending physician has determined that there can be no recovery from such condition and my death is imminent, where the application of life-prolonging procedures would serve only to artificially prolong the dying process, I direct that such procedures be withheld or withdraw, and that I be permitted to die naturally with only the administration of medication or the performance of any medical procedure deemed necessary to provide me with comfort care or to alleviate pain.

In the absence of my ability to give directions regarding the use of such life prolonging procedures, it is my intention that this declaration shall be honored by my family and physician as the final expression of my legal right to refuse medical or surgical treatment and accept the consequences of such refusal.

I understand the full import of this declaration and I am emotionally and mentally competent to make this declaration.

_____
(Signed)

The declarant is known to me and I believe him or her to be of sound mind.

_____
Witness

_____
Witness

Our constitutional right to vote our medical choices belongs to each of us; and whether we or our designated DPAHC voice our decisions, this is one of our most intimate personal choices. This is because it controls the one life we are divinely each given.

Many people are, therefore, doing all they can to enjoy living more, by trying to ensure a dignified death, with proper advance documentation. Some people have even gone so far as to purchase Medic Alert bracelets, such as diabetics wear, as well as people with life-threatening, medically-diagnosed conditions and other allergies. These bracelets are inscribed with, "LIVING WILL/DO NOT RESUSCITATE (DNR), and are worn in hope that their wishes will be respected because they are documented.

The reason people are taking such measures is that they often do not believe that hospitals will honor their wishes. Rather than awaken in an undeterminable condition in a Surgical Intensive Care Unit (SICU) or a Medical Intensive Care Unit (MICU), people want to be granted their right to die a dignified death, without enduring the time, pain and cost that medical prolonging measures encompass. Also, people want to spare their loved ones the emotional pain of having to helplessly watch them suffer.

Older people are especially concerned regarding DNR orders, because of rightfully-feared brain and/or physical impairment—although this condition can be rendered to individuals of any age. However, of sixty-eight elderly patients who received a full cardiopulmonary resuscitation (CPR) effort at a veterans' hospital in Houston, none older than seventy years of age survived. This is but one example as to why the concern of the elderly, especially, is so acute.

When the time arrives in a patient's care for implementation of Durable Power of Attorney for Health Care on behalf of the declarant, there can be real problems and complications when decisions are delayed. The posture of many individuals faced with complex situations is that "time will tell," or "we shall see what we shall see."

Well, in everyday-life situations, as well as life-threatening ones, individuals who cannot seem to face a situation and come to a decided course of action may find they are in for a real shock. "Going with the flow" and "straddling the middle" may be the best course for a jockey who just wants to stay in the race. But if the jockey wants to win the race, the necessary risks must be taken. The price of winning could be the cost of losing. Because just "sitting back" and "taking time to see" what "time will tell" is like the jockey who is just "riding along" like he is in a rocking chair, and not ever really racing or pushing to win. It remains everyone's personal choice of what to do with the time each of us is allotted that results in what is seen that has been done with that time.

This scenario is true with many health-care decisions. It is analogous to not really racing to win, with one tremendous, big difference: In the race of life, it can come as a great shock in learning too late that not deciding is, in fact, deciding.

If a patient or the chosen DPAHC does not refuse a life-sustaining measure, the doctors cannot and do not withhold it. Doctors are obligated by the Hippocratic Oath to err on the side of intervention.

If the doctor's decision is not what the DPAHC agent would have directed, but he or she was "just waiting to see" and in the interim the patient died, the race for life is over, and death is the victor. But what is important here is that your designated DPAHC agent truly understand precisely what you, as the declarant, want done on your behalf.

The question of what is futile, incurable and terminal is boundless. Indeed, we all share a terminal condition: Life!

If you are in a terminal condition, with or without your regular doctor attending your care, it is equally advantageous that all know how you feel, and have signed copies of these documents in your file. Should the need occur to activate your Living Will or DPAHC document, it is so crucial that your designated DPAHC understand, without question, how you feel about specific medical interventions. You need to have fully discussed and given directions to be followed according to situations A, B, and C previously outlined.

While some people choose death, at issue here is not suicide or euthanasia, either passive or active, because both suicide and euthanasia mean ending life. Passive euthanasia is when the patient receives the action that results in the end of his or her life by the cessation of life-supportive measures. Active euthanasia is when the patient participates in the actions that result in the end of their life.

THE POINT HERE IS TO END THE PROCESS OF DYING, and encourage a greater enjoyment of living. Knowing you have implemented all of the safeguards possible for a dignified death, we are therefore able to enjoy life as much as possible.

Alarmingly, the suicide rate of Americans sixty-five and older jumped 21 percent between 1980 and 1986. And updated federal figures for 1990 show a four-percent increase for Americans eighty-five years of age and older. Some encouragement may be felt, however, because there was an eight-percent drop in the suicide rate for sixty-five- to seventy-four-year-old Americans.

Assisting with suicide is a crime in the United States. Yet to attempt suicide alone, whether or not the attempt is successful, is not a crime under U.S. law.

We all are looking through the glass darkly; that is, we see each other only from the outside. So we are all partially blind to one another, even when we have twenty-twenty vision. And, we do not know intimately another person's dreams, crosses, weaknesses or strengths, because the only great common denominator is the thread called Life. Yet, while it can have terrible frustrations, it can be good. Especially, if at the end of our life's charter we still have love, faith, hope and charity intact.

Today, "death" can be defined as:

1.　　The absence of clinically-detectable vital signs.
2.　　The absence of brain-wave activity.

Technology's advancement has brought the development of more sensitive techniques for detecting biological processes, even those which might not be overtly observed. Today, the trend has become to measure "real" death on the absence of electrical activity in the brain, as determined by the process of a "flat" electroencephalograph (EEG) tracing. This is a machine which amplifies and records the minute electrical patterns of the brain.

But, flat EEG tracings have been recorded of people who were later resuscitated. Overdoses of drugs, which are depressants of the central nervous system, as well as hypothermia (low body temperature) have both resulted in this phenomenon.

So a more restricted definition is of death as an irreversible loss of vital functions. Indeed, many people "come back" to tell of near-death experiences that indeed do simulate *Reflections of Life after Life*. This book, written by Raymond A. Moody, Junior, M.D., and the numerous ones on the subject of death written by Elisabeth Kübler-Ross, M.D., bring to human hearts real-life experiences centralized around other's encounters.

The question of futility has also become part of the broader debate over rising medical expenses, and whether some physicians are too quick or not quick enough to use medical technology. This question will surely continue to be debated. The American Medical Association published, in the spring of 1991, new CPR guidelines, recommending that doctors be allowed to unilaterally withhold CPR in futile cases.

However, in the few futility cases that have gone to court, judges have been reluctant to back the physician over the family. But, sometimes, doctors feel they must challenge advance directives in what is called the practice of "good medicine."

Indeed, America has long advanced from the time of families having indentured servants. Doctors are not in servitude of the family whose loved one they are given care.

Physicians and nurses are held responsible for their actions, so they can and do have freedom of choice and authority over their actions to not commit unethical care. Determining what is appropriate care is often not an easy task, even with Living Wills and Durable Power of Attorney for Health Care documents waiting in the wings for possible and necessary implementation to back up caring doctors and staff who become the critically-ill patient's earthly angels of mercy.

People who have endured the battle to keep quality life for their loved one know the agony of the hours of waiting for the scales balancing life and death to tip. When the call to depart or to remain is so close, the hearts of those who love and want the ills of the present to be miraculously dissolved cannot be put in terms of weights and measure.

When health-care junctures and their prognosis, the art of tracking an illness or disease and projecting the outcome, is hanging by a mere thread to life and are not uniformly agreed upon for a dignified death is when facilities, doctors and families sometimes consult.......

CHAPTER EIGHT

BIOETHICS, BIOETHIC COMMITTEES, AND LEGAL BIOETHICS

We have entered a coming of age of bioethics. This is the moral philosophy of life and death. The Patient Self-Determination Act, Living Will, and Durable Power of Attorney for Health Care documents, the increasing number of suicides and suicide attempts and legislative proposals, such as the 1991 Washington State Initiative #119—although defeated to legalize assisted suicide and euthanasia—will surely further propel the proliferation of bioethic committees in hospitals and health-care facilities. These committees implement the task of educating staff members about various moral choices and providing consultation to patients, loved ones, and clinical staff in regard to ethically complex cases. They serve as mediators, helping staff and loved ones come to understanding and agreement about the course of a patient's care.

The deliberations of bioethic committees and hospice are not the same. Hospice is the provision of good medical care for the dying when it is agreed that death is the final result of the patient's illness or disease. The decision had been made by them or their medical proxy to *provide care*—not to *provide treatment*. Hospice affirms the quality of life, always holding fast to the principal of neither hastening nor postponing death.

Hospice can be maintained in the patient's own home or what is termed inpatient hospice. This is a facility that provides highly skilled nursing care and pain relief to the patient in a loving environment devoid of most of the usual medical regulations.

Today's changing technology and the legal constraints of daily life and modern medicine further complicates discussions when trying to arrive at the best decision with consideration of all viewpoints. Definitions of what precisely is curative and palliative treatment can be quite different among reasonable people. Curative treatment, by dictionary terms, is that which is done to help *cure*. Palliative treatment is listed as that which is done to reduce the bad effects of something—to make it more palatable.

No case can be simple when human life and deep convictions are involved. Death is the either/or to life, but surely dying and the process wherein it is facilitated cannot be so readily confined. Living Wills and DPAHC documents should help agents and physicians to understand patients' wishes, so that each is comfortable with the decisions and actions of the other.

However, there are times when medical proxy agents, by delaying, are deferring to physicians. Thus, there are times when physicians avoid acting on agents' decisions: by ignoring or overriding them; by delaying procedures; or by providing information to loved ones in a way that steers agents to accept the physician's decision, when the patient's loved ones are not really comfortable with what is being done.

These are the times when bioethic committees are often most valuable to either side needing an intermediary to facilitate understanding. It is hoped that the process will make the practice of good medicine become the practice of the best medicine. It has been wisely stated that the key operative for complete and full health comes when hearts, mind, and body merge. Then it is possible, through understanding, for there to be real love.

The pre-eminent decision maker ALL THE TIME does not have to be the doctor. Doctors cannot bear the entire burden when dealing with patients. No case is simple. All cases are multi-faceted when human life and deep convictions are involved.

Nurses often know the patient's needs and desires better than the doctor. At the end of the time for earthly care, nurses may today be the primary care provider, with the exception rather than the norm being a loved one. It is most valuable that their insight is utilized in bioethical considerations. Compassionate clergy also afford windows to the innermost desires of the patient.

Medical technology has so advanced that people are kept alive, even when they have lost consciousness and any independent ability to function. Yet, while many patients could just as likely die soon after technological interventions, others often live for extended periods of time. But many patients who do continue to live are so ill that they are not aware of their treatment. They are subject then to what oftentimes would be considered by them unwanted, and sometimes unnecessary, treatment which can unnaturally prolong the dying process. This has categorized doctors in the eyes of many in the role of "playing God."

Yet is it not true that whenever anyone has responsibility, whether assigned or it is just taken by that person, that they become paternal by virtue of the fact that they are saying what someone else will/may or will not/may not do or have done to them.

In terms of patient treatment this has been called "medical Paternalism." Are adults who have "dubbed" some doctors as "playing God" some of the same individuals who, alone, would want the legal right to end life, as the 1991 defeated Washington State initiative would have permitted? If they reach a final decision alone, are they then each "playing God"?

Initiative #119 would have made Washington State the first jurisdiction in the world to authorize doctors to administer lethal injections to incurably ill patients. Many people have misconceptionally thought that the Netherlands and the State of Michigan have already made the procedure legal. This is because assisted deaths have occurred in these locations and have been publicized.

The publicized and documented assisted deaths that have been carried out have not resulted in convicted prosecution, because they came either under "grey areas" of the law or were executed in accordance with existing laws. The Netherlands allowed doctors to assist terminally ill patients to die under strict reporting conditions. This was expanded in February, 1993, to have "mercy killing" legal when death is imminent. But make no mistake, Holland, Sweden and Norway have all kept euthanasia "technically" illegal.

Michigan has erroneously been regarded by some people as a state where suicide-assisted death is legal. This misconception is because of the suicide deaths that were aided by Dr. Jack Kevorkian, a retired Michigan pathologist. Dr. Kevorkian's actions have made him known as "Dr. Death."

In 1990, Janet Adkins, a fifty-four-year-old woman diagnosed with Alzheimer's disease, committed suicide with Dr. Kevorkian's help long before her symptoms were severely disabling. Dr. Kevorkian was charged with first-degree murder.

However, the murder charges against him were dismissed by District 52-2 Court, Judge Gerald McNally, at the preliminary exam. The reasons were that this occurrence came under a previously unrelegated area, and therefore its lawful ambiguous interpretation.

Laws are the rules we choose to live by. Once laws are enacted, it is unlawful to not follow them. But it must be realized that laws follow the need to have them—laws do not lead in advance of their need.

Judge McNally had to give his ruling based on the facts of the actual events and use existing laws to substantiate his judgment. The facts are that Dr. Kevorkian did set up his suicide-assistance machine for Janet Adkins' perusal. However, it was she who pushed the lever to activate the lethal injecture. She was diagnosed with Alzheimer's disease, but was fully aware of the conscious decision she was exercising.

Therefore, the law left undefined his accessory role, as it does the shop owner who sells a gun that the person then uses to accomplish suicide. True, Dr. Kevorkian knew in advance what and when Janet Adkins was planning to do. Yet it was she who, of rational mind, consciously determined and completed the self-execution.

Dr. Kevorkian was barred from further use of his so-called suicide machine which monitors lethal liquid injectures. However, Dr. Kevorkian admits willfully assisting other chronically-ill individuals to use his suicide machine since that time. Once again he was charged with murder.

Dr. Kevorkian acted alone as a physician engaging in these suicide-assisted deaths. He has drawn a great deal of international media coverage because of his openness. All of this has focused attention, therefore, on Michigan as "the place" where "it" "is done," and on Dr. Kevorkian. It has brought before the public the immediacy to really openly debate euthanasia.

Michigan legislators have passed a temporary law, that will lapse in fifteen months, under which it is a felony to participate in suicide assistance. The state, and indeed the nation, will have to review this dilemma and finalize the current law for participation in actions having permanent and irrevocable consequences.

Washington State's Initiative #119 is interestingly named. America knows that to dial 911 will bring help *to save life*, while, conversely, Initiative #119 would have permitted a patient to have a lethal injecture administered *to end life*.

Unlike Advance Directives, either in the form of Living Will or DPAHC documents, Washington State's Initiative #119 aid to dying could be requested only at the time it was to be provided, not in advance. Many controversial questions are at issue.

First, how do we define an incurable disease?

Second, does having an incurable disease necessarily mean that we are going to die from the disease?

Third, what if the diagnosis is a misdiagnosis, but decisive action has already been taken?

Fourth, how is the degree of dependency, pain and disability that is acceptable to one person, but may be unacceptable to another, to be decided, and by whom?

Polls show continued public favor on the side of mercy killing. However, it is not clear if all of the implications for the medical profession and the potential for abuses have been fully considered.

At this time, the American Medical Association (AMA) is against lifting its traditional opposition to physician-assisted suicide and euthanasia.

The AMA's position on this issue, even with Initiative #119's defeat, will hopefully propel respect for bioethic committees. While their deliberations may end in agreement not to further life-sustaining procedures, they can not, at this time, decide upon lethal injections.

Reconciliation of this societal issue will require an adult and open debate of many specific groups within America, as well as the American populace. Religious, medical and legal factions will have to convene for a unifying and satisfying doctrine to be established.

Advance Directives do provide documentation for precisely what they are collectively named. Initiative #119 was structured so that it could not be drafted in advance. Would an optional addendum to advance directives be that if after cessation of treatment death did not result, lethal injecture could be given if so outlined in advance?

Doctors, nurses, loved ones and legal representatives can sometimes find they have come face to face with a patient's death. Although the patient is still living, it is as embodying a personalized looking glass of probable death. It is seen with varying degrees of clarity by each, depending upon viewpoints and emotions. However, the complex realities will make it nonetheless personal for the patient when the mirror of life becomes his or her monogrammed receipt of life's final paper documentation—the death certificate.

Another dimension of these health-care deliberations is termed legal bioethics. This brings the combination of legal doctrines and moral philosophies of life and death together to reach decision for medical treatment.

An example of this would be the dilemma my mother and I faced with my father's days of dying. His Living Will was written according to Virginia statute. However, he was soon to go into a vegetative countdown that, in accordance with Florida statute, gave him no protection by having a Living Will written in accord with Virginia statute.

Therefore, to curtail scheduled major surgery that would have further assaulted his already tortured body, we had an appointment to obtain a court order to legally prohibit this. It is not an uncommon dilemma, nor is it unusual that this sidestep is granted on the patient's behalf.

In our case we felt supportive understanding and had all information and alternatives outlined, but had no statements or unspoken pressures to direct our decisions. This was not a case of an adult's future being decided by medical paternalism. This was a unified effort to have his pre-Advance Directive honored after every medical, religious and family intercedence for his return to full health was fulfilled.

Medical paternalism has been tested in cases regarding children. Drug-related conditions, abnormalities, transferred dependencies and congenitally-contracted AIDs have high percentages in newborn infants.

The position seems to have been in health-care matters involving the imperiled young, especially newborns who have neither a medical history, nor are developed to have expressed any desire in regard to their future life, that parents are not in a better position to know what is best.

Bioethic committees do mediate and facilitate accord among involved parties to exchange viewpoints and agree to a plan of medical care for the patient. Sometimes these decisions become entangled in court legalities, as in the Florida case of "Baby Theresa." The child was born with anencephaly, in which the brain fails to develop beyond the stem, which controls reflexes such as breathing and heartbeat. Death from this condition results within hours or weeks.

The court battle her parents waged to have Theresa declared brain-dead was not granted by a county judge, citing a 1988 state law which says that death cannot be declared until all brain activity ceases. The case was to be ruled upon by the Florida Supreme Court at the time of Baby Theresa's death. The unanswered question that would have mushrooming effects is: How does brain activity cease when there is not a brain?

Courts of law and the court of public opinion are not necessarily simultaneous in their accord. The length of the life that is in balance and the family/medical/legal caretakers' profiles all calculate into the answer of whether to or not to "fight for the death."

A democratic society as ours that has a system of checks and balances offers Americans a choice. The business of dying is not just about mortuaries and cemeteries. Indeed, for those who have lived a "normal" life span it is the conclusion of one's life work. The questions balancing the scales are: Was it a life of contentment? Was it a death of contentment?

Today many choose natural childbirth as a part of a return for environmental embrace of life's beginning. Living a life of contentment and feeling harmony's song of true nurturing enrichment can be one's greatest earth work. For some, this state of living contentment may never be reached. By others, this state is attained almost at birth with seemless effortlessness like a bequeathed life membership that will hopefully be maintained into death.

Our right to choose a natural death, by completing the necessary documents required under state laws, offers the opportunity for the individual to restore to their death its dignity and personal sense of right leave taking. In the first place, some may never want well-meant life-support procedures intruding into their lives. Should they, however, want that assurance, like a life insurance policy will be paid in full when submitted, these documents will be fully followed or administered. Moreover, that they will be granted their choice of life's departure.

Exchanges of joys of the heart make for the whole out of life. We all feel the whisper of eternity in the gentleness of a touch or the breeze.

Sorrows of heartache, in tragedy or another's death, can quickly replace the state of normalcy's routine when it seems impossible to maintain a feeling of wholeness out of the death experience. And yet, we all feel the certainty of eternity in the finality of forever still hands, the rage of wind gales or the final pound of a judge's gavel to declare the law.

These are the yodeling echoes of determining questions each of us need to answer in documented forms before our called departure time. How we answer these questions of ethics and pain are not measured out any less on either side of life's seesaw, whether the life is new or old. The question of what and who is right or wrong is not any the more readily answered.

Living life is not always achieved under ideally contrived conditions. The same is true of dying.

Precise, honest communication expressed by each that is heard mentally, comprehended fully, and emotionally taken into one another's heart and soul with compassionate response is our only hope for love at any time, in living or in dying. This exchange closes the gap between the ideal and the actual.

When the gap between the ideal and the actual is closed, this is what makes what is real take flight, to live or to die, and for all to accept that it is not I who deal out an ideal life. Rather, it is that to each is dealt one life——to live with honor, and to end with a DIGNIFIED DEPARTURE.

GLOSSARY

OF

TERMS AND ACRONYMS

AMA - *American Medical Association.*

ACTIVE EUTHANASIA - *Action in which the subject patient participates that results in his or her death.*

ADVANCE DIRECTIVE - *Term used to collectively refer to Living Will/Treatment Directive and Durable Power of Attorney for Health Care document/Appointment Directive.*

AGE OF MAJORITY - *Term used to qualify being "of legal age" or what is referred to as "adulthood."*

BIOETHICS - *The moral philosophy of life and death.*

CARDIAC ARREST - *When the heart stops.*

CURATIVE TREATMENT - *That which is done to help cure an individual.*

CYANIDE - *Very poisonous chemical substance that comes in different forms: hydrocyanic acid; nitroprusside; potassium cyanide; and sodium cyanide.*

DECLARANT - *Person making a verbal or written statement.*

DNR (Do Not Resuscitate) - *Means do not resume the breathing process and beating of the heart.*

DPAHC (Durable Power of Attorney for Health Care Document) - *An inclusive legal agreement that permits the person* *appointed as the designated agent to fulfill your health care wishes, should you become terminally ill or in a persistent vegetative state. This is also referred to as an Appointment Directive.*

ELECTIVE HEALTH CARE PROCEDURES - *Medical care that the patient chooses to have done, such as the dental procedure of a "root canal," but which is not life threatening if not done.*

EEE (Electroencephalograph) - *A machine which amplifies and records the minute electrical patterns of the brain displayed on a graph tracing of this activity.*

EMERGENCY TREATMENT - *Medical care that is given a patient under life-threatening conditions requiring prompt actions and immediate decisions which will only later be determined whether or not correct based upon the results.*

FUTILITY CASES - *Case where treatment produces no results for the subject/patient.*
HCFA - *Health Care Financing Administration.*

HEALTH CARE PROXY - *A designated agent to act on behalf of another individual in health-care matters, if they become unable to do so. It is often included within a Living Will and may, like a Living Will, have limitations. For example, it may only cover terminal illness, which would not include a coma or Alzheimer's disease.*

HHS - *Health and Human Services.*

HIO - *Health Insuring Organization.*

HMO - *Health Maintenance Organization.*

HOSPICE - *Term used to qualify good medical care for the dying when it is agreed that death will be the final result of the patient's illness and that the patient wants care, not treatment.*

IMMUNIZE - *To have special exemptions from penalty or infection.*

INPATIENT HOSPICE - *A facility that provides highly skilled nursing care and pain relief to the dying patient in a loving environment devoid of most of the usual medical regulations.*

LEGAL BIOETHICS - *The combination of legal doctrines and moral philosophies of life and death decisions in determining medical treatment.*

LW (Living Will) - *Document that outlines medical treatment you do or do not want at such time should you no longer be able to express your wishes. This is also referred to as a Treatment Directive.*

MICU - *Medical Intensive Care Unit.*

MEDICAL PATERNALISM - *Using the science of medicine as distinct or separate from surgery to set the policy of governing or controlling people in a paternal way—providing for their needs, but giving them no authority.*

MERCY KILLERS - *Desperate people who "unilaterally" kill others in the belief it is the only compassionate thing to do.*

MIRANDA RIGHTS - *The constitutional rights that police routinely recite to those they arrest.*

MURPHY'S LAW - *Principle that whatever can go wrong, will go wrong.*

PALLIATIVE TREATMENT - *That which is done to reduce the bad effects for an individual.*

PASSIVE EUTHANASIA - *Action done for the subject/patient that results in his or her death because of the cessation of particular life-supportive measures.*

PATIENT AUTONOMY - *When the patient is self-governing.*

PSDA (Patient Self-Determination Act) - *Law to strengthen the role of patients in health care decision making.*

PERMANENT VEGETATIVE STATE - *A condition in which one survives indefinitely without recovering.*

PERSISTENT VEGETATIVE STATE - *A condition in which the subject/patient is unable to respond to his or her surroundings and is not really aware of anything, even though the eyes may periodically open. It is similar to a coma, in that the person is unresponsive, but it is a permanent or persistent condition.*

PROGNOSIS - *The art of tracking an illness or a disease and projecting the outcome.*

SICU - *Surgical Intensive Care Unit.*

SURROGATE - *A substitute.*

TERMINAL CONDITION - *A state caused by injury, disease or illness from which to a reasonable degree of medical probability there can be no recovery, and death is imminent.*

TERMINAL ILLNESS - *A condition in which death is imminent in a matter of days or weeks.*